W9-AFE-401

THE POCKET ENCYCLOPEDIA OF
AGGRAVATION

THE POCKET ENCYCLOPEDIA OF
AGGRAVATION

97 Things in Life That Annoy, Bother, Chafe, Disturb, Enervate, Frustrate, Grate, Harass, Irk, Jar, Miff, Nettle, Outrage, Peeve, Quash, Rile, Stress Out, Trouble, Upset, Vex, Worry and X, Y, Z

YOU!

By Laura Lee

Illustrated by Linda O'Leary

Tess Press

Copyright © 2001 Laura Lee
Original Artwork © 2001 by Linda O'Leary

All rights reserved. No part of this book may be reproduced in any form or by any electronic or
mechanical means including information storage and retrieval systems.

This edition specially printed for Barnes and Noble by Black Dog & Leventhal.

Published by Tess Press, an imprint of
Black Dog and Leventhal Publishers, Inc.
151 West 19th St.
New York, NY 10011

Cover design by Scott Citron
Interior Design by Scott Citron

Cover photograph from Imagebank

ISBN: 1-57912-341-4

h g f e d c b a

Table of Contents

ACKNOWLEDGEMENTS

Thank you to my unofficial research assistant Cal Lee and to the many friends who sent me lists of their pet peeves. My friends and acquaintances, it turns out, are annoyed by so many little things that they didn't all fit. To editor Will Kiester who has the irritating habit of making me work harder and write better. I hate that. Thank you to Linda O'Leary who did the brilliantly annoying artwork. To Scott Citron for creating the book's "look" and everyone at Black Dog & Leventhal who came up with ideas on how to make this book just a little more aggravating.

I am eternally grateful to a few people who have been there whether I'm celebrating the release of a new book or feasting on ramen noodles and black beans (it's yummy, really). First, to my parents, Albert and Carol Lee, who would have less aggravation if their daughter had a nice secure day job, my brother and best-friend Cal and his wife Jennifer Lee, my non-related best-friend Jenny "Nick" Hunter and to Lisa Guthrie and Joanne Carpenter who offered a respite this winter between calls from Citibank, Discover, Blue Cross, Chase Manhattan.... (See also credit card debt.)

"I said to myself, Arlo, if you were dead, a lot of the stuff that pisses you off probably wouldn't bother you so much."
—Arlo Guthrie, introduction to the song *Wake Up Dead.*

Introduction

"You know what's really aggravating?" In the past several months, while working on this book, I have not had a single conversation that did not contain this phrase. Now that the book is out, I doubt things are going to change. People are frustrated by thousands of little things from hangnails and papercuts to the mother of all aggravations—telemarketers.

No one is immune. On several occasions, the experts I consulted—scientists with long titles and multiple PhDs—ended our conversation by ranting about those little threads that hang from sweaters, people chewing on pencils and fitted sheets that don't.

For example, I contacted Dr. Ron Grassi, D.C., M.S., DABDA, FACFE, Diplomate American Boards of Forensic Medical Examiners & Physical Disability Analysts, with a question about why stiff necks hurt so much. (An entry which, incidentally, did not make the final cut. Sorry about that.) Along with my answer I got the following: "Why do people

scream on cell phones like they're yelling across a canyon? They don't do this on a regular phone. How about someone scraping the ice cream bowl with a spoon (after there is hardly any left) while you're lying in bed at night watching a movie. And the DOOR SLAMMERS!!!!! Do you know how insulting that is to a Corvette convertible?"

Other experts were not as amused by the concept. A representative of Rensselaer Polytechnic Institute seemed a bit annoyed when I phoned to ask if there was a mechanical engineer who could explain why a hand-held can opener slides off the rim, leaving that little bit of joined metal that you can't seem to cut through when you start with the opener again. (I never did get an answer to that one.) One local librarian was confused when I came in and explained that I was looking for the psychology books because I wanted to find out why two pedestrians trying to get out of each other's way both dodge to the right, then both dodge to the left, and end up doing an odd sidewalk dance. "You're not going to find any books on that," she said with a squint that clearly indicated she was sure I was insane or making fun of her or both.

The idea for a book on life's little aggravations came to me one afternoon in August. I was sitting beside a pond, lazily contemplating the way the sun reflected off the ripples in the water, when my reveries were interrupted by the itchy poke of a mosquito boring into my left arm with her sipper. My mind was filled with questions. Why do mosquitoes flock to me more than to other people? What makes that lump appear on the skin? What makes it itch? Why are there annoying things like mosquitoes on the planet, anyway? It occurred to me that other people must wonder about this kind of thing as well. Why do I keep losing socks in the wash? Why am I always in the slowest line at the supermarket? Is there a correct answer when the cop asks, "Do you know how fast you were going?"

"Little things punctuating our lives on a daily basis cause the most stress," Allen Elkin, program director of the Stress Management and Counseling Center in New York, once said. "Small insults come at us faster than bigger problems, hit us more frequently, seldom let up and quickly accumulate."

Not only that, we love to talk about them. Psychologists used to think this kind of venting released our frustrations. Now they think the opposite, which means writing this book was probably bad for my health. How aggravating is that?

I'll admit it, months of focusing on aggravations did get to be a bit negative at times, but overall the experience has been positive. As the author of a book on aggravations, I've been able to turn negatives into positives. "I got a paper cut. Hey! That's annoying!! Yes! Another entry!"

On a larger level, the fact that Americans are obsessed with the dust on their computer monitors and legroom on airplanes is a good sign. You can only muster the energy to get upset about these things when the outer world is in a state of relative peace, tranquility and prosperity. Although I have not found statistics to back it up, my guess is that scientists spend much less time and energy trying to figure out the exact chemical composition of intestinal gas or how long it takes a cookie to turn to mush in your mug when the nation is in the midst of war, famine, plague or economic depression. In the absence of a huge national crisis, we have the freedom to ponder the little things. In that spirit, this is a highly uplifting work.

There is no escape from aggravation. People who live and work in cities deal with smog, long lines, traffic jams, noise, crowds and a more fidgety, tension-filled lifestyle. People who live in the country have their own annoyances: bugs, road-kill, stepping in cow dung and having to drive 20 minutes to get to the nearest post office. Some people choose to work in offices, where they deal with difficult co-workers and bosses, uninspiring environments of office cubicles, and having to plan months in advance to get days off. Others avoid those hassles by being self-employed. They deal with self-employment tax, paying for medical insurance out of pocket and not having a weekly paycheck. People who live alone have to pay all the rent and there's no one at the house to call for help if the car breaks down. People who live together have to compromise more. I have come to the conclusion that the key to life is choosing which annoyances you prefer to deal with and adjusting your lifestyle accordingly.

I fully expect to receive angry letters from telemarketers, airline food service workers and the creators of Barney. Believe me, I'm sympathetic. I used to be a mime. Annoyances are subjective. One person's noise is another's symphony. One's aromatherapy is another's loud perfume. I compiled my original list of annoying things from personal observation and suggestions from friends and acquaintances. If I had written entries for all the items on my master list it would rival the Oxford English Dictionary for shelf space. For some reason, my publisher thought that might make it hard to sell. Aggravating. I reduced the list by focusing on the aggravations that seem to elicit the most venom, and those that have the most interesting explanations. Belly button lint, stubbed toes and bird droppings on a car are annoying, but there is little mystery to why they happen. For me, the biggest aggravation of all is that this is not a book that I can ever feel is finished. There are only so many pages and only so much time, and there will always be extra aggravations worthy of mention that simply don't make the cut. Plus, we keep inventing new and better aggravations (see improvements that make things worse). The other annoying thing is that, for some reason, an inordinate number of annoyances seem to start with the letter "C" and I couldn't think of anything annoying that starts with Q. What are you going to do?

ACADEMIC LANGUAGE THROUGH **ARMREST WARS**

ACADEMIC LANGUAGE

"Since thought is seen to be 'rhizomatic' rather than 'arboreal,' the movement of differentiation and becoming is already imbued with its own positive trajectory."–*The Continental Philosophy Reader,* edited by Richard Kearney and Mara Rainwater. The line is part of an introduction intended to help students understand the chapter. Sure. That explains it.

Why do academics insist on writing in language that makes the reader squint and develop a headache? It is simply a matter of style, say defenders of dense, challenging prose. Different forums have different rules. *People* magazine has a different style from the *New York Times,* which has a different style than the *Sears Catalog.* Every profession has its jargon. Academic specialties have more than their share because they are expressing complicated and often new ideas.

"There's a kind of presumption among journalists and people who talk about culture in the media that if it's written by an

Brain processing complicated concepts

Unintelligible prose

English professor, it should be comprehensible to others," Dr. Eric Mallin, an associate professor in the English department at the University of Texas at Austin, told the *Dallas Morning News.* "That's assuming there is no specialized knowledge particular to the field."

Dr. Judith Butler, professor at the University of California at Berkeley, was unwittingly thrust into the center of the academic writing debate when the New Zealand publication *Philosophy and Literature* awarded a 90-word sample of one of her articles the top prize in its annual Bad Writing Contest. The "honor" is given to the most "stylistically awful sentence" to come out of the scholarly world.

Butler defended her style of writing in a *New York Times* op-ed piece. Academic writing needs to be "difficult and demanding," she said, in order to question concepts that are so ingrained no one thinks to question them. Having to think about the meaning of each sentence provokes "new ways of looking at a familiar world."

Others believe the jargon has little to do with communication.

They see it as something akin to a secret handshake or a series of multisyllabic passwords. It is written to confirm academic authority, membership in the club.

In 1996, a New York University physicist submitted an article with fake phrases and gibberish to the journal *Social Text,* which published it as genuine scholarly analysis. When an English professor at Southern Oregon University was asked to paraphrase a long sentence from the Bad Writing Contest's second prize winner, he admitted, "It doesn't make a lot of sense to me."

Yet to gain tenure, professors must publish, and to be published, they must adopt the accepted style. Philosopher Bertrand Russell summed it up in his essay "How I Write." "I am allowed to use plain English because everybody knows that I could use mathematical logic if I chose," he wrote. "I suggest to young professors that their first work should be written in a jargon only to be understood by the erudite few. With that behind them, they can ever after say what they have to say in a language 'understanded of the people.'"

ACNE

When you reach that special age when you start to think about trying to attract a boyfriend or girlfriend, you become preoccupied with your appearance—just then Mother Nature reveals she has a sick sense of humor. Your skin begins to change, an oily sheen covers your face and pimples pop up everywhere. What is more, the stress of having acne can give you acne!

The tendency to get acne is inherited. Males are more prone to it than females during their teenage years, but because it is hormonally triggered, adult women often have outbreaks of acne that correspond with their menstrual cycles. Scientists speculate that this side effect of puberty once had a purpose. In the days when people hunted and foraged for food in the wild, the skin may have needed extra protection from the elements as we reached adulthood. Now the over-active oil glands just give you zits.

Androgens, the sex hormones released at puberty, cause the

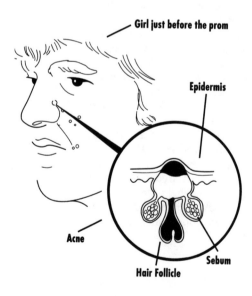

Girl just before the prom

Epidermis

Acne

Sebum

Hair Follicle

production of sebum, the fat that naturally keeps your skin and hair soft. Somehow, though, the sebum gets trapped along with dead skin cells. The follicle stretches outward and a bump forms on top. Contrary to popular belief, blackheads are not caused by dirt that gets stuck in a pore. Blackheads are oil plugs that make their way to the surface and turn dark when the air hits them. If they are covered and can't break through the surface, the oil plug stays white.

When the sebum in the blocked gland is transformed into free fatty acids they become food for bacteria. The body responds by sending white blood cells to kill the intruders. The result is pus and a big pimple.

The tendency to get acne couldn't come at a worse time in life. David Elkind, who studied egocentrism in adolescence, showed that during our teen years we become preoccupied with our self-image. We feel there is an imaginary audience watching our every move—an audience full of critics. Stress—having a big test, a job interview, a big date or an outbreak of acne at a time when you feel especially self-conscious—causes your body to release more androgens, which can trigger new pimple outbreaks, which can cause more stress, which causes your body to release more androgens...

As if having your face erupt before the big date isn't upsetting enough, some acne medications may cause depression all by themselves. Accutane, an acne treatment, has been cited by the Food and Drug Administration as having depression as a side effect. Its manufacturer denies this allegation, claiming that it is the severe acne, not the treatment, which causes depression in teenagers.

AIR TRAVEL DELAYS

See also armrest wars, legroom on airplanes

The Gannett News service says if a flight is 45 minutes long, you can expect your journey to be about four hours when you consider checkin, takeoff,

carry-ons, sitting in loud waiting areas and trying to sleep in chairs.

In 2000, one out of every four flights was delayed, canceled or diverted, according to the Department of Transporta-

Line for takeoff

landing, collecting luggage and leaving the airport. When you add in a delay due to weather conditions in Timbukthree, your 45-minute flight could end up as an entire day of lugging heavy

tion (DOT). The average delay, including sitting in the terminal and waiting on the tarmac, is 50 minutes.

You can blame some of the tardiness on the weather. A storm that socks in Chicago's O'Hare can screw up schedules around the nation. Of course, the airlines could solve some of this by allowing a little more breathing room in their schedules. According to *Newsweek,* The Dallas-Fort Worth airport can handle 35 flights every 10 minutes in perfect weather. The airlines, however, schedule 57. So even on a bright, sunny day, at least 22 planes are going to be delayed.

Then there is the antiquated air traffic-control system. David Fuscus of the Air Transport Association told *Newsweek,* "It's 1999, and we still have a 1970s system." He added, "I wouldn't want to imply it's all 1970s. Some of it is 1960s."

The Federal Aviation Administration (FAA) needs to have a margin of safety that allows for glitches and equipment problems. Controllers are instructed to leave a cushion of as much as 60 miles between aircrafts, compared with the mandated 5 miles.

There are a few things you can do to sidestep delays such as fly early in the day. One delayed flight can cause other flights to be delayed. By the end of the day, you're far more likely to have to wait. You can also check flight statistics on the DOT Web page: www.bts.gov/ntda/oai. There you can see which airlines and airports have the best on-time performance.

Remember DOT's Rule 240: In the event of any flight irregularity—with the exception of bad weather—the original airline must endorse your ticket to the next available flight on any airline. Nine of the 10 major U.S. carriers accept one another's tickets. Southwest is the hold out.

Try to keep your temper on the ground. The more people shout at airline employees, the more irritated and short tempered they become themselves. Pretty soon the skies are rather unfriendly. That doesn't help anybody.

"When people are stuck in traffic in a cab, do they get angry at the cab driver?" Continental Airlines chairman Gordon Bethune asked *Newsweek.* "We don't want to sit there any more than you want to sit there."

AIRLINE FOOD

See also air travel delays, armrest wars, legroom on airplanes

"Punishment for small children." That's how Ed Stewart described Southwest Airlines food to *U.S. News and World Report*—and he's their spokes-man! Southwest spends about a quarter per traveler on meals.

Since 1992, airlines have been serving cheaper and cheaper meals—if they serve meals at all. In 1992, if you bought a domestic or international seat

Chicken?

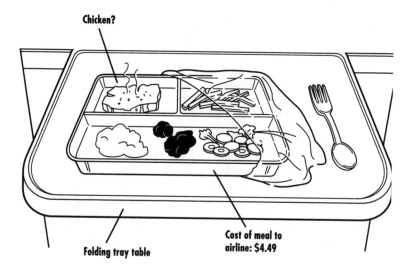

Folding tray table

Cost of meal to airline: $4.49

you got a meal that cost on average $6.11. By 1998, the cost of the meal had dropped to $4.49.

In 1999, Delta downgraded their food service on 140 flights. They replaced sandwiches with snacks such as cheese and crackers. On 160 flights that had snacks, they now just give beverages. Why are they doing this to us? Maybe they're trying to make us skinnier so we'll fit into those cramped seats, or possibly, they are trying to save a little money—about 14 million little dollars a year.

The world's largest caterer, LSG-Sky Chefs, did a survey to find out just how important food service is to the average traveler. For international flights, 31 percent of the survey respondents said that food service was the most important reason they chose a particular airline. When it comes to those short domestic hops, only 12 percent choose a carrier because of its menu.

Most of us choose our airlines based on low ticket prices. If Delta offers a four-star meal and ups the ticket price and American offers a bag of peanuts and gets you to Florida less expensively, American will win out. The airlines say they're doing their best to give you the best meal $4.00 can buy.

That money we think we're saving on airline tickets? We're still spending it, and airport food courts are the benefactors. The *Wall Street Journal* reports that the food courts racked up $1 billion in food and beverage sales, thanks to a growing number of passengers who carry meals on with them.

If you need more information on airline food you might enroll in England's University of Surrey, which is home to the first professor of airline food. The University, located 20 miles from Gatwick Airport, offers courses in in-flight catering.

A

ALUMINUM FOIL AGAINST DENTAL FILLINGS

You sit down to lunch at the office and carefully unwrap a ham sandwich from a sheet of aluminum foil. Unbeknownst to you, a small piece has remained in the sandwich and when you bite into your lunch the foil is pressed between your fillings. A sharp pain vibrates through your teeth, as if a sadistic dentist were trying to inspire a Pavlovian fear of ham on white. The pain is literally an electric shock.

Dental fillings are made of mercury combined with either tin or silver. The aluminum foil acts as

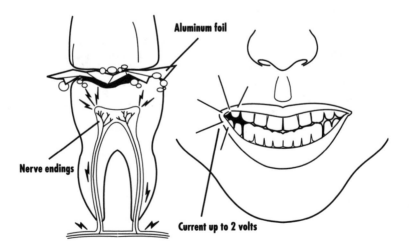

Aluminum foil

Nerve endings

Current up to 2 volts

an anode, the filling as a cathode and your saliva is an electrolyte "salt bridge." The result is a galvanic cell, which releases an electrical current of up to two volts. Believe it or not, at least one researcher says chewing on tinfoil is good for you. According to the Wireless Flash News Service, researcher Miklos Gombkoto of the Hungarian Dental University of Gyor did a month-long study in which 20, presumably broke, Hungarian college students agreed to chew aluminum foil for 30 seconds, three times a day for $75. Gombkoto reported that the electrical charge helped kill germs in the mouth that cause bad breath and tooth decay. Feel free to experiment on your own.

ANNOYING COMMERCIALS, OR "YOU'VE GOT RING AROUND THE COLLAR!"

"Vern! Hey Vern!" "I've fallen, and I can't get up!" "It slices, it dices, it juliennes, call in the next half hour and get an extra knife absolutely free! Now how much would you pay?"

They shout at you, cajole you. They have grating voices, inane

catch phrases and nag you about things like ring around the collar, knocks and pings, black heads and that little itch that could be telling them you have dandruff. You already have a mother, thank you very much.

You'd think advertisers would do everything in their power to get on your good side. Not so. Advertisers today have quite a task to get your attention. Every day the average American is bombarded with 600 to 1,200 commercial messages. The Big Four networks are increasing the amount of time they give to advertisers. During an hour-long show you'll see 11 minutes and 12 seconds of commercials, up from 9 minutes and 38 seconds in 1991. When you add in the network's own promotions for upcoming shows, you end up with 45 minutes of drama and 15 of pitches. When you figure in print ads, billboards, messages on plastic bags and Internet banners, you probably see about 3,000 ad messages every day. If you happen to go to the mall, another 10,000 plugs will be sent your way.

In the same way that stepping on a piece of glass is more memorable than stepping on a feather, a commercial that insults your intelligence, rattles your ears or otherwise annoys you, is more likely to be remembered.

Some of the finest examples of the annoying genre came out of the 1970s when our attention spans were just starting to get really taxed. That's when Ron Popeil came on the scene. His Ronco direct television spots were made with a shoestring budget. Popeil wanted to use every second of his $7.50-a-minute time so he spoke as fast as he could, edited out pauses for breath and sped the whole thing up mechanically. The hyper pitch sold Veg-O-Matics, Mr. Dentist, the Pocket Fisherman and Mr. Microphone "Hey baby, I'll be back to pick you up later!" The commercials presented a problem and an

"as seen on TV" product that was the solution.

"Play this game with yourself," Popeil told the Palm Beach Post. "Pick any object on your desk. First, come up with a scenario of all the problems that product solves. Then introduce the product. Then show how the product works. Then tell the customer how to buy the product. Do that in 30 seconds' time, and it sounds like someone's trying to shove this thing down your throat."

Another company, Dial Media, followed in Ronco's footsteps. They took a knife and gave it the Japanese-sounding name Ginsu. To the hyper hard-sell they added a new twist, freebies. Buy a Ginsu knife and you get a cleaver, a bread knife, table knives—but wait, there's more!—a set of spoons. These folks were the forerunners. They blazed a trail for today's infomercials and home shopping networks. Let's face it, if they weren't presented to you on late night TV would you ever think you needed a Chia Pet, the Clapper, spray on hair or a singing robot fish? Now how much would you pay?

ANTS

See also cockroaches, fleas, flies, gnats, mosquitoes

Ah spring. The flowers grow once more, the sun shines...and your kitchen is suddenly swarming with ants.

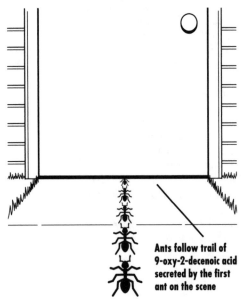

Ants follow trail of 9-oxy-2-decenoic acid secreted by the first ant on the scene

They're everywhere, and they just keep coming.

Why do ants suddenly appear in such large numbers in spring? Over the winter, ants stay in their underground nests. They subsist on the stores of food they collected over the summer. When it gets warm, the population swells and the workers head out once again to collect nourishment. A crumb that is barely noticeable to a human is a tasty feast for an ant.

According to the trade magazine *Pest Control,* homeowners now rank ants ahead of cockroaches as their biggest insect headache. It's good news for them. They call ants the industry's most "economically important pest." Still, ant control seems to be "starting from ground zero," Dr. William Robinson, president of Urban Pest

Control Research & Consulting, reported.

Most of the ants you see indoors are female workers who live in colonies outdoors. If you observe them for long, you will see that they are marching to and from a food source and carrying nourishment out of your home back to the queen. When a worker ant comes across food, she starts secreting 9-oxy-2-decenoic acid from an abdominal gland. Other ants follow it and reinforce it with their own trails. As the food is exhausted, the ants stop secreting and the trail dries up. They are so guided by the scent that if you were to wipe your finger across it and create a break in the path, the ants traveling in both directions would come to a complete stop.

Poisonous sprays are strangely satisfying, but they don't work in the long run. You get to see a few worker ants fall on their backs and die, but the poison never makes it back to the queen. As soon as their friends find the way back, you'll see ants again.

There are other reasons to avoid sprays. As many as 500 species of the most common household insects are now resistant to

many of the most widely used insecticide according to Sheila Daar, executive director of the Bio-Integral Resource Center in Berkley, California. They can still be dangerous to humans, especially children.

Ant traps work by offering a supply of poisoned food in a dosage small enough to make it back to the nest. If the baits are too strong and you see dead ants around it, leave them where they are; eventually, other ants will take their corpses back to the nest where they will poison the colony. Dead ants have their own pheromone, 10-octadecenoic acid. Ants treat a dead peer as if it were living until they smell the acid. Then they take the body to the dead ant dumping ground. If you put the acid on a living ant, the other ants will pick it up and dump it as well. The discarded ant will return only to be carried off again until the acid evaporates.

Instead of spraying, see if you can figure out where the ants are coming from. You can block the entry with a glob of petroleum jelly or toothpaste. Then clean up their path with soapy water. This will eliminate the chemical trails the scouts left for other workers.

ARMREST WARS

See also inefficient sidewalk pass, office cubicles, standing too close

You're next to a big man on a long airplane journey. The insensitive, space-hogging guy has his oversized limb on the armrest. This is completely rude and unfair because you want the armrest to yourself. Without making eye contact, you wedge your elbow behind his. With each bump, you try to jostle your arm a little bit further forward, but his arm has become as stiff as a board. No way is he giving up. His muscles may cramp up, but his hairy forearm is going to be on that armrest until someone pries it off.

Psychologists call the areas of disputed personal space "ambivalent zones." Whether or not you get into a confrontation depends on who is in the adjoining seat. Our bubble of personal space expands or contracts depending on how we feel about the other person. If it's a friend, family member or someone you're attracted to, you probably won't have a problem.

When it is a stranger, the battle lines are drawn. We rarely come to blows over the invasion, or even discuss it. We just reposition ourselves and try to slide our arm into the space. This is because we react to personal space violations by trying not to acknowledge the invader as a person.

Who wins the war? Not a woman. If a man sits beside a woman, odds are five to one that he'll take the armrest. Dorothy M. Hai and her team from the St. Bonaventure University School of Business observed men and women on commercial airline flights and found that a man takes up more space regardless of whether he is bigger or smaller than the woman.

The researchers followed up by interviewing about 100 of their subjects. They learned that travelers were fully conscious of the elbow war, even if they behaved as if they weren't. They were surprised to discover that young men who lost the armrest to women expressed more anger than their elders.

"I feel I deserve to have it," one young man told Hai. "She doesn't."

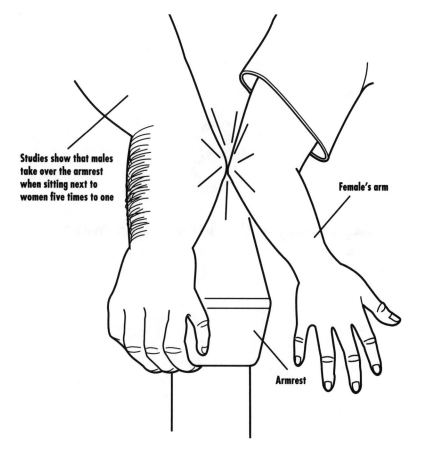

Studies show that males take over the armrest when sitting next to women five times to one

Female's arm

Armrest

BAD BREATH THROUGH **BOOMING CAR STEREOS**

BAD BREATH

See also aluminum foil against dental fillings, dentist's drill

Breath test: Do people recoil when you exhale? Have you bought stock in Listerine? Do you spend more than 10 percent of your income on mints? Does the dog run away? Has your breath killed small houseplants? You could be one of the estimated 25–85 million Americans plagued by bad breath, also known as halitosis or "foetor oris."

"Bad Breath is a problem that originates in the mouth," Dr. Jon Richter told *Men's Health* magazine. It seems obvious enough, but lately a slew of television ads have promoted pills that supposedly fix your breath problem from the inside out. They don't work. Ditto the $1 billion a year we spend on mouthwashes, breath mints, sprays

and gums. Those will reduce the odor for an hour at best.

You probably don't like to think about it, but your mouth has an ecosystem all its own. To a microorganism, your mouth's 95 degree temperature and high humidity is like a Hawaiian par-

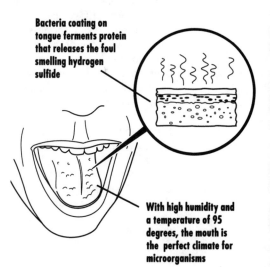

Bacteria coating on tongue ferments protein that releases the foul smelling hydrogen sulfide

With high humidity and a temperature of 95 degrees, the mouth is the perfect climate for microorganisms

adise. More than 400 different species call it home. You feed them every day when you feed yourself. Some of the sugar and carbohydrates stay behind providing a bacterial feast.

The tongues of some people become coated with bacteria that ferment proteins. The fermentation process produces methylmercaptan, fatty acids, ammonia and hydrogen sulfide. This last gas is responsible for the sulfur odor of bad breath. (A similar fermentation process takes place in the intestines: *see farts*)

No matter how much you brush and floss, your morning mouth probably smells more of sulfur than spearmint. Over night the microorganisms that inhabit your mouth have several hours to eat and break down food into amino acids and peptides with their stinky byproducts unmolested by a toothbrush.

Even if you refrained from brushing for the same number of hours during the day, your breath would not smell like it does in the morning. During the day you talk, chew and swallow. These activities help keep the saliva flowing.

Saliva, it turns out, is pretty amazing stuff. It keeps the eco-system in your mouth in balance. It contains bicarbonate ions that buffer the tooth-decaying acids produced by bacteria like S. mutans (see *dentist's drill*). It also contains phosphate and calcium ions, which repair microscopic cavities. It is full of antibacterial agents and proteins that cause bacteria to stick to each other so they can't stick to the surface of the tooth. The saliva then washes the bacterial clumps away.

During the night, saliva production drops off and its antibacterial action stops as well. The organisms multiply, coat your tongue and wait for you to get up and grab your toothbrush.

If you seem to have foul breath no matter how much you brush, you probably have what dentists call a "geographic tongue." This means your tongue has more indentations than other people's. This gives anaerobic bacteria extra places in which to live and multiply.

The best way to keep your breath fresh is to clean the back of your tongue. You don't need to buy a fancy tongue cleaner—use an inverted spoon to gently scrape the back of the tongue then rinse.

BARNEY

See also TV always on

Barney got run over by a tractor
Best of all it happened on Tee Vee—
All the little children are unhappy
And I am just beside myself with glee
　　—lyrics to the tune of "Grandma
Got Run Over By a Reindeer," circulated on the Internet.

Few, if any, beloved children's characters have inspired the kind of loathing that PBS's purple dinosaur Barney has. The star of the two-to-three-year-old set made his debut in 1992. By 1993 retailers were selling about $500 million worth of licensed merchandise. *Forbes* magazine ranked Barney as that year's third highest earning entertainer with royalties and gross earnings of around $84 million. That year also marked the height of the new sport of Barney Bashing. "I Hate Barney" Web sites and news-letters proliferated. Some shopping mall Barneys were quite literally bashed. While Barney's popularity has waned slightly from his 1993 heyday, the show is still highly rated. Kids still love it. Adults still hate it, and many hate it with a passion. What is it about Barney that makes grown-up jaws clench?

It could be the production values, which, in the words of *People* magazine, "make *Mr. Rogers' Neighborhood* look like *Beverly Hills, 90210.*" Or perhaps it is corny new lyrics sung to the tune of familiar songs like "This Old Man." Maybe it is the program's unrelenting positiveness and lack of conflict that grates on adults dealing with real-world challenges. While programs like *Sesame Street* were designed to entertain parents while the children watched, Barney is written exclusively to please children.

As Barney creator Sheryl Leach told *People* in 1993, "We write the program for kids only, on one level. We feel it's important that parents approve of Barney, but it's not important to us that they be entertained." Parents forced to watch hour after hour of Barney with their delighted toddlers may simply suffer from overexposure to an icon they were never meant to appreciate.

Adam Cadre developed another theory as he was researching generational polemic at UC Berkeley. He believes the backlash is a case of the generation gap in action. Parents of today's youngsters are largely from the cynical, alienated, go-it-alone Generation X, a "reactive generation." Barney preaches team spirit, community and conformity. "These are the kind of values, both positive and negative, associated with the civic personality," he writes. "The fact that the children of the nineties are both growing up on Barney and actively choosing to watch him strongly suggests the generational cycle has finally moved out of the reactive phase and into the civic phase."

Barney is written to please children without regard for parent's entertainment

Kid having fun

Barney the purple dinosaur on TV

BLARING COMMERCIALS

See also annoying commercials, noise, overplayed music

It's 2AM and you're in your pajamas watching a *Charlie's Angels* rerun. You don't want to wake the folks in the neighboring apartment; your walls of course, are made of plywood. Farrah and team just got their instructions from Charlie and suddenly the volume goes through the roof: "I'M CRAZEEE EDDIE AND MY PRICES ON APPLIANCES ARE INSANE!" You dive across your coffee table towards the volume control, breaking an expensive vase and cracking your head on the floor as you trip and fall. This is it, you think, death by endorsement.

You probably did that leap for nothing. Your senses tell you the advertisers are cranking up the volume on commercials, but there's a good chance your senses are not giving you a full picture. The Federal Communications Commission (FCC) regulates the frequency and volume at which a station can broadcast. The top decibel recording of anything on television can only reach a certain legal limit.

You're not alone in thinking the commercials are louder. The FCC gets complaints about it every year. In 1997, for example, 275 people complained about the volume of commercials. The agency has looked into it and in 1984 they put the issue to bed saying there was nothing they could do about the "apparent loudness" of commercials.

The reason commercials appear to be louder is twofold. First, you're not as thrilled about listening to commercials. Unpleasant sounds tend to seem louder. The other reason is that commercials pack more sound into their legal limit than shows do.

In a typical movie, sitcom or news show, the volume has peaks and valleys. A love scene comes through your speakers at a different level than a shoot out. Advertisers can't afford to be subtle. So they fill the valleys and broadcast with all peaks.

"Imagine the soundtrack like a cup," David Perry of the American Association of Advertising Agencies told the Associated Press. "The FCC decides how tall the cup is. We decide how much we put in the cup. The programs give you coffee. We tend to give you pea soup."

TV manufacturers are trying to solve the problem by installing automatic volume levelers on their sets. They are designed to control the volume from show to show, station to station and program to commercial.

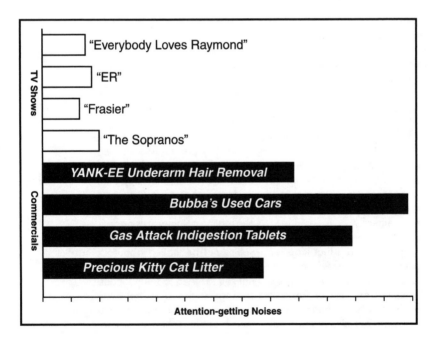

TV Shows

"Everybody Loves Raymond"

"ER"

"Frasier"

"The Sopranos"

Commercials

YANK-EE Underarm Hair Removal

Bubba's Used Cars

Gas Attack Indigestion Tablets

Precious Kitty Cat Litter

Attention-getting Noises

BOOMING CAR STEREOS, OR THIS IS YOUR BRAIN ON NOISE, ANY QUESTIONS?

See also annoying music, blaring commercials, car alarms, noise

Boom, Boom, Boom, Boom... I'm trying to sleep here! Boom, BOOM, BOOM, Boom... Your teenage son's car has been fitted with super-mega-mondo-killer-ultimate-platinum bass speakers. When they're cranked up—which they always are—the car shakes, glass breaks, dogs howl and small animals run for cover. Your son just bops his multiply pierced head in appreciation.

Boom-cars are primarily a male obsession. The most devoted enthusiasts of booming music spend thousands of dollars on their audio systems and enter their souped up cars in competitions. So far, the loudest car stereo competition winner blasted in at 155.5 decibels, more than twice as loud as a jet taking off and definitely loud enough to cause permanent hearing damage. It only takes about 115 decibels to do that. Emergency sirens, at 120 decibels, don't stand a chance against the loudest boomers.

Robert Franner, editor of the Toronto-based audio trade publication *Market News,* once compared sound level competitions to "comparing genitals. It's overkill for people with naturally occurring high levels of testosterone."

Franner may not be too far off. Young males use their booming cars to draw attention, mark territory and to draw the attention of females. Recent research shows that a boom car is something of a sexual stimulant on wheels. A 2000 study by England's Manchester University found that loud music stimulates a part of the ear that is con-

B

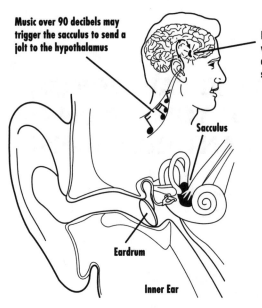

Music over 90 decibels may trigger the sacculus to send a jolt to the hypothalamus

Hypothalamus which controls desire for food and sex

Sacculus

Eardrum

Inner Ear

nected to the brain's pleasure center.

The sacculus, a tiny organ in the inner ear, is part of the system that controls the sense of balance. It does not appear to serve any function in hearing, but it does send messages to the hypothalamus, which controls the human appetite for food and sex. The sacculus is sensitive to sounds over 90 decibels, which may send a kind of pleasure jolt to the brain.

"The distribution of frequencies that are typical in rock concerts and at dance clubs almost seem designed to stimulate the sacculus," Neil Todd, who led the research team, told *New Scientist.* "They are absolutely smack bang in this range of sensitivity."

The pleasure may be addictive. Researchers at Northeastern University in Boston identified what they call Maladaptive Music Listening. People who suffer from MML can't seem to stop listening to loud music even when it is literally deafening. Deprived of a daily loud music blast, the subjects suffered withdrawal symptoms including depression, moodiness and lethargy.

CAR ALARMS THROUGH **CRINKLING CANDY WRAPPERS**

CAR ALARMS

See also booming car stereos, noise

It's 3AM. You are in the middle of that dream where you are flying over your childhood home when EEAAAEEEE-AAAAEEEE...It's your neighbor's car alarm. Do you A.) Rush outside to foil the robbery in progress. B.) Immediately call the police. C.) Put

Annoyed woman

EEEAAAEEEAAAA

Car alarm

DLX6

Bump by purse

your pillow over your head and mutter "@#$% car alarms."

Chances are, you picked C. Separate studies in both New York City and Los Angeles show that 95 percent of the alarms are false. Smaller cities nationwide have had similar results. People feel more secure when they have alarms. Our quest for peace of mind has created an industry with sales estimated at $473 million a year.

That's $473 million worth of 129-decibel wailing noise boxes. How loud is that? The average crowd noise at a Redskins football game is only 89 decibels. Ninety decibels is the legal limit that the Occupational Administration allows for an eight-hour work day in an industrial setting. A chainsaw is 100 decibels. Above 115 decibels, noise is hazardous within minutes. At 180 decibels, sound waves are so strong the body literally heats up. (Car alarms only seem like they do that.)

The wail is not only loud, it is designed to grate. It is high-pitched with repeating multi-tones. A typical siren has six tones so it can be customized. Apparently in urban areas there are so many alarm-equipped vehicles, and they go off so often, no one recognizes the sound of his own car being invaded. To make it easier, alarm makers have made it possible for consumers to choose exactly what ear-splitting combination of tones they want.

Yet New York City councilmen say there is no evidence that audible alarms deter auto theft. Experienced thieves can make off with your vehicle in a matter of seconds. For police officers, false alarms go beyond annoying. The International Association of Chiefs of Police estimate that false alarms—both home and auto—cost police departments as much as $600 million per year in added manpower. If they weren't following up on cars that were brushed by passersby, there would be an extra 60,000 police to foil real crimes.

One Los Angeles cop confessed that he put a car alarm only one step higher on his priority scale than "a car blocking a driveway." Everyone knows it, so no one pays much attention to the shrill sound—at least not as a warning. It is still very effective as a sleep deterrent.

C

CATS SHREDDING FURNITURE

Some people have nice furniture—people without cats. You, on the other hand, have sofas with vertical rips that bleed stuffing. Sure, Fluffy is cute when she purrs, but when she scratches your furniture to bits you want to take about eight of her nine lives.

One of the reasons a cat scratches is to peel the old sheaths off the nails. Scratching also seems to be a form of exercise. Yet the most important reason Fluffy claws away may be to mark her territory.

The domestic cat has not strayed far from its wild origins. She may seem like a cuddly household pet, but in her mind, she is a big game hunter. In the wild, a cat has a large territory, depending on its gender. Males patrol about 150 acres and females about 15 acres. They are looking for food and mates and trying to keep other cats away from their food and mates. Since you give your cat all the food she needs, and she has been spayed, she shouldn't need to obsessively mark and guard her personal space—but she still does.

T.S. Eliot got it right when he wrote a poem about the cat that was "always on the wrong side of the door." You let Fluffy out, two minutes later she is scratching at the window demanding to be let in. Two minutes after that, she is meowing at the door, ready to go back out.

"Cats are very territorial animals," says Betsy Lipscomb, president of Cats International. "They have to investigate every square inch of their territory. They have to patrol it on a regular basis. Wherever their little paws have walked, that's now their territory. If the door

C

is closed—they've been in that room before, they want to go in there and check it out on a regular basis. That's why they hate closed doors. It interferes with their job. They have a great duty."

Your cat requires the assistance of your opposable thumbs to get to the other side of that door, and she would rather have your begrudging help than wait around to check if there's a hideous beast lurking in part of her territory.

"Felines in general are dominant creatures," says California veterinarian Petra Drake. "Big cats such as lions and tigers are all basically at the top of the food chain with very little real threat of predator action against them. With this level of domination, big cats are able to exert tremendous control over their environment. Their movement in and around their territory is at will and constrained only by whim. Take this genetic endowment of environmental control and place it into a ten pound feline then stick in it a domestic setting. You get a wonderfully entitled creature who refuses to be constrained by a simple mechanical door handle."

The scratching is part of this primitive impulse. It not only leaves a visible mark, it also leaves an odor for other cats to smell. The scent is secreted through glands in the cat's paws. This is why declawed cats keep trying to scratch. They are still able to spread their scent.

To change Fluffy's habits, you'll have to doctor your furniture for a little while. You can try putting double-faced masking tape on the corners of the furniture or covering the entire piece of furniture with a sheet. Where you put the scratching post is also important. Put it near the thing the cat most loves to destroy.

Scratching helps to peel old layers of nails off claws

Fluffy

Your favorite couch

CAUGHT IN TRAFFIC

" **I** just want to get there! Just let me get there! I just want to get off this road!"

By the time we get to work, our blood pressure is up, we're too tired and irritated to function well, and we're more easily frustrated. Raymond Novaco, a professor of psychology at the University of California at Irvine, has been studying the negative effects of commuting for more than 15 years.

"Regardless of age, income, race or social position, red lights and crowded freeways make us frustrated," Novaco told *Prevention* magazine. "We found that the longer the commute, the higher the blood pressure."

Novaco's team also found that those with long commutes had more work absences due to colds or flu. Plus, long commutes create more pollution, which

contributes to all our respiratory distress. About 40 percent of smog is due to auto emissions.

Urban sprawl and increasing traffic congestion mean commuters are spending more time behind the wheel. Each day 100 million Americans buckle down for an average 20 minute commute. About 13 percent of us spend 45 minutes or more just getting to our places of employment.

The traffic situation is worst around cities, of course. Almost half of the nation's total population lives in one of 39 metro areas. Between 80 and 90 percent of the population in those areas drives a private vehicle to work. If you live outside Los Angeles, traffic jams are a way of life. It was rated the most congested urban area in 1994 followed by Washington D.C., San Francicso-Oakland, Miami, Chicago, Seattle and Detroit.

It is New York, however, that invented "gridlock." The term came into common use during a transit workers strike in 1980. It sent so many commuters out in their cars that Manhattan's street grid was paralyzed—locked, i.e. for one car to move one car length in downtown Manhattan, one car had to exit the island uptown.

Road congestion is not likely to end in the near future. Evidence suggests Americans are not so much seeking solutions to the problem of traffic as finding newer and better distrac-

tions to entertain us during what we see as inevitable commuting doldrums. Manufacturers of cellular phones, electronic games, computers and television sets hope to mine the demand for in-car entertainment. Delphi president J. T. Battenberg says the market for auto electronics will grow from $300 million in 1999 to $5 billion in 2003.

And that's not the worst of it. We may soon see frustratingly long commutes combined with off-key singing. *Men's Health* reports a Japanese car-maker is already offering optional in-car karaoke. Telecommuting is looking better and better.

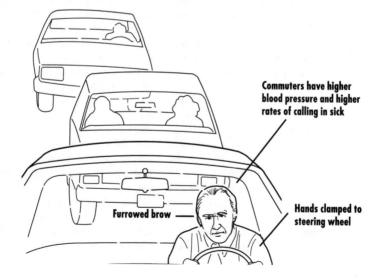

Commuters have higher blood pressure and higher rates of calling in sick

Furrowed brow

Hands clamped to steering wheel

C

CD SKI..I..I..I..I..P

See also booming car stereos, noise, overplayed music

"Hey, turn it up, this is my favorite song!" you say, but your snapping, singing and good mood abruptly stop when Hanson's MMM-Bop (that *is* your favorite song, right?) is replaced by something that sounds more like Pac Man eating the same dot over and over and over. That's when you discover that a compact disc makes a great Frisbee.

If you're old enough to have a collection of vinyl discs in your attic, you remember some of the irritations of that medium—the hisses, the pops and the dreaded skips. With the passing of the LP, we may lose the expression "you sound like a stuck record," but fortunately for compilers of annoyances, skipping music appears to be here to stay.

With a compact disc, there is no needle, no instrument at all, in fact, that touches the surface. Thus, the most aggravating vinyl skip pattern, pattern, pattern, pattern, pattern... zzziiipp.. the repetition of a single phrase, is generally avoided. (We won't even mention the 8-Track tape's irritating habit of cutting a song in half and finishing it on another track. Clunk-a-clunk-a-clack.) CD players still skip but they do so in their own unique fashion—a weird robotic sound.

If you look closely at a compact disc, you will see that there is a metal layer coated with clear plastic. A CD burner literally burns peaks and valleys into the metal. Depending on the sound, it burns a pit or leaves it unscathed. These imprints correspond to the zeros and ones of binary code.

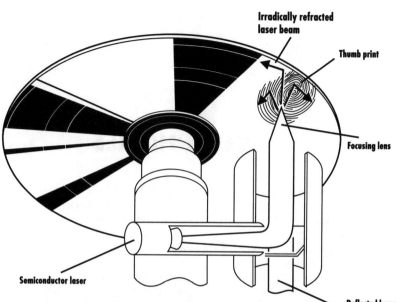

Irradically refracted laser beam

Thumb print

Focusing lens

Semiconductor laser

CD PLAYER SKIPPING OFF THUMB PRINT

Reflected laser beam back to photodiode array which reads the signal

The information runs in one continuous spiral starting in the center of the bottom (non label) side and reeling out toward the edge. In all, the string of data is about three miles long. The CD spins at 500 revolutions per minute. A laser beam, with a width of 1.7 microns (1/14970 of an inch), reads the information by either scattering in a pit or reflecting off a non-pitted surface. Fingerprints, scratches and dirt can all reflect the beam in odd directions and trick it into producing a sound that is different than the artists intended. CD players, like their LP-playing counterparts, are also susceptible to skips when the player is jostled.

Fortunately for music lovers, most CD problems are easier to remedy than those associated with LPs. Often a good cleaning is all it takes to sort things out. If the scratches just nick the surface of the plastic layer, there are machines that can grind them out and make the disc good as new. If a scratch goes down to the metal, however, it's time to buy a new copy of *Pet Sounds*.

CELL PHONES

See also improvements that make things worse, your call is very important to us

Recently Laurence Fishburne made headlines, not for his acting ability, but for his temper. He stopped in the middle of a Broadway performance of *The Lion in Winter* and called out to a member of the audience whose cell phone had been ringing for 20 seconds: "Will you turn off that [explicative] phone please?" The audience applauded wildly.

Cell phone users seem to have no sense of place. They shout into their phones (for the same reasons people shout when wearing headphones) in the middle of concerts, theatrical performances and funerals. Behind the wheel they're a menace. According to a University of Toronto study, car phone use is as dangerous as drinking and driving. It's not having your hands off the wheel that is the culprit, it is the conversation that keeps your mind occupied so you forget to slam on the brakes when that five year old chases a ball in front of your vehicle.

Yet drivers do a lot of frightening things. We complain much more about the dangers of cell phone use than, say, riding a motorcycle without a helmet. That is because we still see cell phones as something of a status symbol. A team of Liverpool, England, psychologists recently concluded that men in that country use their cell phones the way a peacock fans its feathers—to impress the females of the species. The novelty of cell phones is quickly wearing off, but people still feel important when they use them. As sociologist Jill Stein once put it, "Now everybody gets to be a big shot."

We see a person who swerves in traffic because she is chatting on the phone or who interrupts your quiet meal with an annoying ring as more than rude. They think they're more important than the rest of us. Therefore, a cell phone slight makes us angrier than other social faux pas. That is—when *other* people do it. A recent survey by SBC Communications, makers of Cellular One and Pacific Bell products, showed that cell phone users rated most wireless phone users a C, D or F for manners. They consistently gave *themselves* an A or a B.

Many sociologists believe that the problem will clear itself up. New technology comes along faster than we are able to create rules of etiquette for it. Eventually, we will reach enough social agreement that few people will step out of bounds. In the meantime, here are a few tips. For safety's sake, do not talk on the phone while driving. If you must make a call, pull off the road, even if you have a hands-free phone. For the sake of other's nerves, don't talk on the phone in a restaurant or theater. If you must take a call, go outside. And if you're bothered by people talking loudly near you, you might try the suggestion of the Chicago commuter who discourages his fellow travelers by pulling out a notebook, leaning in and taking notes of their conversations. Works every time.

Gentleman watching performance

Cell phone ringing

C

CHEWING GUM POLLUTION, OR GUMFITTI

You're on your first date with the cute red-haired guy you've had your eye on for weeks. He takes you to a sidewalk café. You're both smiling and chatting pleasantly until you cross your legs and the knee of your silk slacks gets stuck to the table by an oversize wad of dirty chewing gum that someone parked underneath. Not only are your slacks ruined, but the expletives coming out of your once sweet, feminine mouth have ruined any chance that you'll ever have children with freckles.

Americans didn't invent chewing gum. According to London's *Independent,* a university researcher named Elizabeth Aveling concluded from tooth marks in prehistoric tar that children have been chewing gum in northern Europe since about 7000BC. We have certainly taken to the habit, though.

In fact, if the jaw power Americans use chewing gum could be harnessed, it could light a city of 10 million for a year. We spend $2 billion a year on 83 billion sticks. Modern chewing gum is made out of 40 to 50 compounds including pine-tree resin, petroleum products, wax and synthetic latexes. You're basically chewing a stickier version of the stuff they use to cover golf-balls. It doesn't go away, so when the sugar and flavorings have disappeared, the gooey lump has to go somewhere. It's surprising we're not all stuck in place from the gum on the soles of our shoes.

Recently in Milwaukee, a frustrated city alderman threatened to hold up part of the city budget if something wasn't done about the gum on the sidewalks. If you take a good look at a city sidewalk you'll see black spots. That's ground-in, dirt-encrusted, already-been-chewed gum. It's expensive and time-consuming to remove. You can freeze it with Freon and scrape it up, smear it with citric acid–based chemicals and wait for it to dissolve, try to melt it away with hot water and chemicals or "power-wash" it with pressures of 2,000 pounds per square inch. Sometimes this process damages the pavement without getting up the gum.

Gum is so sticky it almost defies the laws of physics. It is, in fact, about 10,000 times stickier than theoretical models say it should be. Chewing gum, like adhesive tape, owes its stickiness primarily to the van der Waals force, an electric force that acts between uncharged molecules. When experimenters measured the amount of energy needed to pull a metallic probe off a sticky surface, however,

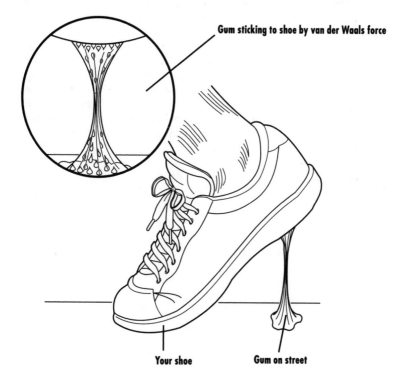

Gum sticking to shoe by van der Waals force

Your shoe   Gum on street

they discovered it took more force than would be needed to overcome van der Waals.

A pair of French researchers set out to find out why. Cyprien Gay, a physicist with the Centre National de la Recherche Scientifique in Paris, and Ludwik Leibler of Elf Atochem, a French Chemical company devised a model that explains chewing gum's sticky behavior.

When your shoe comes down on a piece of chewing gum, the boundaries of the rubber sole and the gum's surface come together. Air is trapped between them. As you pull your shoe away, the bubbles are stretched. They behave like tiny suction cups, which makes it harder to pull the gum away from the shoe and the shoe away from the gum.

There have apparently been no national studies as to how widespread the problem of gumfitti is, but the success of the Gumbusters gum removal company might give you some idea. The company, an import from the Netherlands, started doing business in the states in 2000 with branches in Washington D.C., Atlanta, Tampa, Philadelphia and Dallas. In just four months, Gumbusters' CEO reported that with limited advertising they'd had more than 1,200 service inquiries and 680 inquiries about opening a franchise. Of course, there is an easier way to keep public places clean– throw your chewed gum in the trash!

CHILDREN'S STORIES OVER AND OVER AND OVER AND...

How many times does your child want you to read him *Clifford The Big Red Dog?* About 57 more times than you want to read it. Your daughter, meanwhile, wants to see her favorite video, *The Little Mermaid,* for the 96th time. Parents have been known to "lose" books, to suddenly "forget" how to read or speak English or to "accidentally" back over the video with the car...five times in a row.

Listening to the same story over and over is part of the process that builds the neural pathways that form memory. As Peter Ornstein, professor of psychology at the University of North Carolina at Chapel Hill explained in *Parenting* magazine, "The narrative form is the scaffolding and support for remembering."

The first time a child hears a story or sees a movie, he starts to connect the elements of the story to other experiences. Thus he creates new neural connections, but the connections are tenuous. To build stronger connections, he must reinforce it by repeating the experience.

Child 3–8 years old

Tattered children's book

Little Red Ridin Ho

Father

"The child gets to connect these experiences with other kinds of experiences they've had by watching it over again," says Mary Mindess, director of the Center for Children, Families and Public Policy at Lesley University in Cambridge, Massachusetts. "It makes those neural connections stronger and therefore able to branch out and make other kinds of connections. The story for them becomes more powerful each time they hear it."

There is also an emotional component. Favorite stories evoke strong emotions, joy, excitement and catharsis. Children want to feel those emotions again, and they know they can do so by hearing the same story.

"Young children like to have a sense of power," says Mindess. "The more they can hear the story, the more they can act the part of the story that gives them an additional sense of what they want to try to accomplish. Adults have more avenues for getting the repetition of the same emotional experience than the child has. The child doesn't have as many avenues to seek out, so he likes the repeat of things because he's pretty sure he knows what's going to happen."

The bad news is, there's not really anything you can do to rush through this stage of development. So buckle down and read Green Eggs and Ham one more time. The good news is, they do eventually grow out of it, and one day the book you couldn't stand to pick up will fill you with affectionate nostalgia.

COCKROACHES

See also ants, fleas, flies, gnats, mosquitoes

You're trapped in your bed at night, afraid to step down and walk into the bathroom because there in the dark is your own personal horror movie. Hundreds of scuttling creatures, their feet making tiny clicks. If you dare turn on that light, you will see them zipping off into the corners and under the furniture. Even when you can't see them, you know they're there, somewhere, just waiting.

Cockroaches have been around for 350 million years and have evolved into about 3,500 separate species. They're hearty and highly adaptable. They have developed resistance to many household insecticides. They eat everything from grease spots to mold to each other, and they can get by without food for weeks. A female German cockroach, the species you're most likely to encounter in your kitchen, needs to mate only once. She is able to store enough sperm to fertilize all the eggs she will produce during her nine-month life span and produce about 200 offspring. Some other species can reproduce without even mating through parthenogenesis—pro-

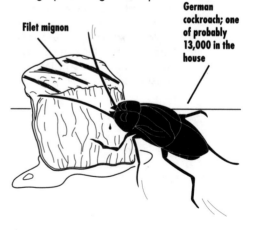

Filet mignon

Female German cockroach; one of probably 13,000 in the house

duction of offspring from unfertilized eggs.

Philip G. Koehler, a professor of urban entomology at the University of Florida, conducted a survey of about 1,000 urban apartments for low-income tenants. Half had more than 13,000 cockroaches each. Heavily infested dwellings can contain 30,000 or more. Yet humans still hope against hope that we can wipe them out. Americans alone spend $1.5 billion a year spraying for cockroaches.

In case you needed a good reason to be grossed out by roaches, newly hatched German cockroaches survive the early days of life by eating the waste of the grown-ups. They never seem to lose a taste for excrement: Older cockroaches eat their neighbors' waste. Researchers at the University of Florida-Gainseville

have found that roaches find their way by following trails left by other roaches that defecate as they travel.

Assuming you do not want to share you home with roaches, one of the least toxic pest control chemicals is plain boric acid. Roaches haven't yet developed resistance to it. Put it into crevices, under sinks and appliances to keep the bugs at bay. If you prefer to avoid pesticides, try putting petroleum jelly on the inside of the mouth of a glass jar and putting bread inside as bait. The roaches fall in, but the jelly makes it too slippery for them to get out.

When roaches die, their legs stiffen and they fall sideways. They have a flat body with a high center of gravity, which is why they roll over when they keel over and you find them on their backs.

COMMON COLD

It's not a big deal, it's just a cold. Not even worth calling in sick. You will just sit at your desk and hold your nose with a Kleenex while you fight the headaches, fever and chills.

Different people have different reactions to colds. Most people, 95 percent, who are exposed to the rhino viruses that cause a cold do become infected, but only 75 percent get any symptoms. People who are lucky enough not to feel sick fight off the infection just as well as you do with your runny nose and endless sneezing. Lucky them. Your dog and cat are immune to colds as well. The cold is only common to humans, chimpanzees and higher primates. Feel better?

Cold viruses can live for a short time on a surface, say someone's hand. Shake hands with that person and you get the

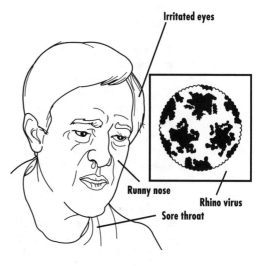

Irritated eyes

Runny nose

Sore throat

Rhino virus

cold on your hand then you rub your nose and voila, the process begins. As little as a single particle of the virus is all that is needed to mount an infection. You breathe in and the virus, which contains strands of genetic coding coated in protein, is transported to the back of the nose by the nose itself. There it attaches itself to a receptor, which transports it into a cell in the respiratory track. Once it's in its cell, the virus can reproduce. More and more virus particles are created until finally the host cell bursts and the dose of viruses infects new cells and the process starts anew. The whole thing takes about 8-12 hours.

It takes about 10 hours for the body to start mounting its defense. The inflammatory mediators histamine, kinins, interleukins and prostglandins cause your blood vessels to dilate so they can transport water and other materials needed to create extra mucus. Mucus is your nose's defense to just about any irritant. Unfortunately, the cold that it is trying to flush out is hidden away safe within the walls of a nasal cell most of the time. However, the sneezing, coughing and nose blowing do have one effect— they help to spread colds to other people.

There is some truth to the old wive's tale about chicken soup. If you're all stuffed up, it will loosen things up a bit; that is the conclusion of three clinicians who published the article "Effects of Drinking Hot Water, Cold Water and Chicken Soup on Nasal Mucus Velocity and Nasal Airflow Resistance" in the medical journal *Chest*. Hot chicken soup increased mucus velocity from 6.9 to 9.2 mm per minute, a result that is "statistically significant" compared to cold water and hot water. The faster the mucus velocity, i.e. how much mucus is expelled from the body, the faster the infected cells are expelled from the body (and spread to other people). The researchers concluded, "hot chicken soup, either through the aroma sensed at the posterior nares or through a mechanism related to taste, appears to possess an additional substance for increasing nasal mucus velocity." Go tell your mom she was right.

COMPUTER VIRUSES

See also computers, internet flaming

Your computer is behaving strangely. Very strangely. You delete a file, and it seems to pop up again in another directory. Delete it again, it reappears somewhere else. There were a few documents in one file that you can't find anywhere now. What's going on? Suddenly a message pops up on your screen, "Super Hacker Strikes Again." You forgot to update your virus scanner's database, didn't you?

Being attacked by a computer virus is like being robbed or

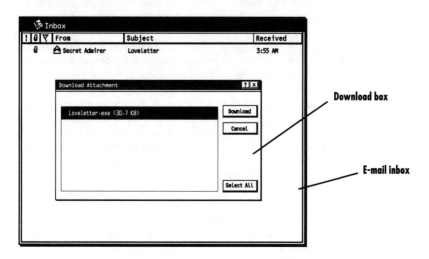

Download box

E-mail inbox

having your windows broken by a vandal. You feel violated, even if the virus did little damage. If it deletes files, rewords important documents or causes your computer to crash, it can have far-reaching consequences. Computer Economics, an independent research firm, estimates that the economic impact of virus attacks around the world came to $12.1 billion in 1999 and $17.1 billion in 2000; and how do you put a price on the damage if the file that was erased was the only copy of your novel or a business proposal?

What type of sick, evil mind creates a program whose only purpose is to replicate itself and cause havoc? "People with pimples," says Dr. Peter Tippett, president and CEO of the Internet security firm ICSA Inc. That is, people aged 17 to 27, for the most part. Researchers have encountered virus writers in their 40s, but most are young pranksters and almost all are male.

Susan Gordon, a leading authority on computer viruses best known as an anthropologist of the cyber-hacker culture, has found that the typical virus writer is middle class with normal ethical development in other areas, i.e. they are not common criminals. The anonymity of the computer world, however, allows them to see the targets of their creations as the machine rather than the human computer user. Teenaged virus writers don't usually have malicious intentions; they say they do it "because they can." Adult virus writers are more likely to have malicious intentions. They talk politics and see themselves as fighting an "enemy" or something that is wrong with society as a whole. Most virus writers are seeking recognition. A virus that is successful enough to make the anti-virus lists or better yet—the news—is a great success for them.

If you can read the code of the virus, you will find that most viruses are personalized in some way. The programs contain comment lines. Normally such lines are used by software designers to describe what the various parts of the program do. Virus writers use them to pass messages along. Sometimes they are rude messages about former girlfriends or the original target of the virus, sometimes just hacker names.

"I think the idea of making a program that would travel on its own and go to places its creator could never go, was the most interesting thing for me," said a Bulgarian virus writer known as Dark Avenger in an interview with Gordon. "The American government can stop me from going to the U.S., but they can't stop my viruses."

The commentary can be helpful in tracking viruses to their authors. Virus chasers examined the programming style and comments in the Melissa virus and compared them to comments made in online discussions and traceable records of Internet access to help track down that virus's creator.

Despite the warnings about viruses that erase your hard drive, render your computer unusable and stop the earth spinning on its axis, most viruses are fairly benign, but still take up time and resources to expunge. Even the most successful viruses—that is, those that spread the fastest—actually employ very simple code. They rely on human nature to propagate them. The recent strain of e-mail viruses send themselves out to the people in the victim's address book. The message appears to come from a friend, grabs the recipient's attention and compels them to execute an attachment they wouldn't run if it came from a stranger.

One such virus, Loveletter, was, in the words of psychologist and consultant Robert Edelman, "sloppily written, but still the most successful combination of psychology and technology we have seen to date."

Various technological solutions loom on the horizon. IBM and Symantec have teamed up to develop a constantly evolving "digital immune system" that will automatically identify possible viruses, find those distinctive signatures and send defenses out to client's machines in less than an hour. Susan Gordon also suggests adding units on computer ethics to high school computer classes.

In the mean time, to outsmart the pranksters, use a secure operating system like UNIX or Windows NT, and alternatives to Microsoft Office. Virus writers want their creations to spread to the widest possible audience, so they program for the most popular software. If you don't want to take that route, install a virus scanner and update its virus tables regularly. Finally, never run a program that comes to you in e-mail unless you are sure you know what it is.

COMPUTERS AKA "THIS @#%$& MACHINE!"

See also computer viruses, improvements that make things worse, internet flaming, power-pointization of the nation, unsolicited bulk e-mail

Computers make us angry, very, very angry. Two 1999 surveys reveal the extent of our rage. In Britain, a survey by the London-based opinion firm MORI for Compaq Computer revealed that 46 percent of computer users were frustrated because they couldn't understand computer error messages. Twenty-one percent said they had missed work deadlines in the past three months because of computer problems. Fourteen percent said computer glitches interrupted their work more than once a day. On the BBC website, computer users in large numbers admitted to swearing at their computers. Meanwhile, on this side of the Atlantic, Concord Communications of Marlborough, Massachusetts, discovered that 83 percent of network managers reported that users had become abusive—kicking computers, smashing monitors and breaking keyboards.

Why are we swearing, kicking and generally abusing our machinery? Psychologists believe we're kicking our computers because we can't kick our bosses, co-workers, clients, parking attendants and small yapping dogs. In other words, we're frustrated with our job responsibilities and we have no outlet for the rage except an inanimate object. Donald Gibson, an assistant professor of organizational behavior at Yale University, blames the increased responsibilities that employees have had since computers came into our lives. Machines that were designed to simplify merely increased our expectations of how much we should accomplish in a day. Meanwhile, companies improve the bottom line by getting rid of employees. The remaining employees can cope with the extra burden as long as the computers are working perfectly. A delay can throw everything off, leaving the employee overwhelmed. More than one news report has featured a man who got so angry with his computer that he took a gun to it.

If you do plan to have an altercation with your computer, here's a safety tip: Don't put your fist through the monitor. Like a television, computer monitors have vacuum tubes that can explode. Beat up on your keyboard instead. It's durable and cheaper to replace.

C

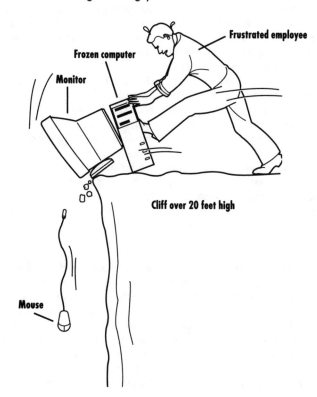

Frustrated employee

Frozen computer

Monitor

Cliff over 20 feet high

Mouse

COOKIE MUSH AT THE BOTTOM OF YOUR MUG

Cookies taste great when they're dunked in hot coffee, but leave them in the liquid too long and they crumble and end up as tasteless sludge at the bottom of your cup, depriving you of your sweet and ruining your morning pick me up. McVites, an English cookie manufacturer, studied the phenomenon and determined that about one quarter of the cookies that are dunked into hot liquid end up as glop. In the process it splashes coffee in your face and all over your clean white shirt. Try to retrieve the cookie and you burn your fingers, spill the whole mixture on your lap and spend the rest of the afternoon greeting clients as a mess of brown stains and bandages.

If you like to dunk, you'll be glad to know that researchers from the University of Bristol in England, after a two month study employing high-tech equipment, have discovered the mathematical formula that determines the ideal dunking technique and time to maximize the cookie to mush ratio.

Dr. Len Fisher and his team, being British, whimsically insist on calling cookies "biscuits" and focus primarily on the dunking of a crisp "digestive" style confection into tea rather than the sensible American practice of dunking more porous (and tastier) chocolate chip cookies into coffee. Still, the scientific principles are the same.

Whatever you call them, cookies are starch held together by sugar. (Ok, so maybe "cookie" is actually a more whimsical term than "biscuit.") When a hot liquid enters its pores the sugar melts and the structure becomes unstable. As this occurs, 10 times more flavor is released than when you eat a dry cookie.

That's why we do it. But, as Fisher told the BBC, "you have got a race between the dissolving of the sugar and your biscuit falling apart and a swelling of the starch grains so that they stick together, giving you a biscuit which is purely starch but rather softer than what you started with."

To determine the perfect dunking time, Fisher coated a digestive in 24 carat gold so he could scan it with an electron microscope and reveal its internal structure. Then he wet the cookies on one side and filmed the progress of the tea as it seeped in. Finally he used an Instron machine to measure how much the biscuit was affected by the moisture.

Using a mathematical formula—the average pore diameter in a cookie is equal to four times the viscosity of the hot liquid, multiplied by the height the liquid rises squared, divided by the surface tension of the beverage, multiplied by the length of time the cookie is dunked—Fisher determined that most English-style biscuits should remain in a hot drink for 3.5 seconds. He also revealed the perfect dunking technique. Using a wide-brimmed mug, the cookie should be dipped at a shallow angle

and after the dunk, it should be rotated 180 degrees so the dry side supports the wet side.

Of course the timing will be slightly different with the softer cookies we prefer on this side of the Atlantic. Fortunately for us, Fisher plans to publish a table which defines the ideal dunking times for various types of cookies.

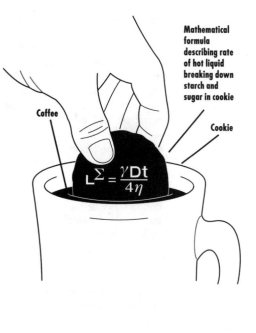

Mathematical formula describing rate of hot liquid breaking down starch and sugar in cookie

Coffee

Cookie

$$L\Sigma = \frac{\gamma Dt}{4\eta}$$

COUGHING IN THE THEATER

See also cell phones, crinkling candy wrappers, laser pointers

You're simply trying to hear the orchestra. Hack, hack, cough, cough, wheeze. Violins. Hacking. Cellos, throat clearing. Brass and phlegm. It bothers the performers too. At a recent concert by the Carnegie Hall Jazz Band in Minneapolis, the musical director, Jon Faddis, stopped and chided audience members for their coughing.

In 1975, the Dallas Opera performed *Tristan und Isolde* and Jon Vickers, as Tristan, was lying flat on the stage while another singer was trying valiantly to be heard over a virtual cough concert. Vickers had enough and shouted: "Shut up with your damn coughing!"

The singer Marilyn Horne once observed that the worst coughing occurs in cities with sunny climates, such as Dallas and Miami. In cities with long spells of damp, cold weather, the audiences are quiet.

Psychology may be as much to blame as itchy throats. During dramatic moments, when the audience is rapt, coughing subsides. When the crowd becomes restless, the coughing resumes. Sometimes though, you just get that tickle in your throat and there's not much you can do. Many theaters have taken to providing free cough drops, but then there's the problem of unwrapping them.

There's a trick to coughing in a theater without making noise. According to Florence B. Blager, chief of speech pathology and audiology service at the National Jewish Center for Immunology and Respiratory Medicine in Denver, you should not stifle the cough, but let the air explode outward. When you feel the cough begin, blow air through tightly pursed lips. This gets rid of the air a cough would expel without going through the vocal chords. We haven't tried this ourselves, but Blager insists it can be done with a little practice. If you don't develop this skill, Judith Martin, author of the syndicated "Miss Manners" column, says if you cough more than three times you should leave the theater.

CRACKING KNUCKLES

If you have a friend or co-worker who habitually cracks his knuckles, you would probably like me to tell you that it causes cancer, AIDS, ozone depletion and nuclear war. Anything that would scare the person enough to make him STOP. Sorry, I can't help you.

What happens inside the hands of a person who cracks his knuckles may be damaging to your nerves, but it's not particularly damaging to the knuckle cracker. Each joint is surrounded by fluid which fills the gap between the bones. Ligaments surround the whole thing and hold the joints together. When you put pressure on your finger, the pressure drops between the bones and the ligament is pulled in by the small vacuum. At the same time, gas is forced out of the knuckle forming a bubble. The bubble takes up the space between the bones, and the lig-ament snaps back into its original position with the familiar popping sound.

Contrary to popular belief, habitual knuckle cracking does not cause arthritis or deformed joints. As Dr. Dave Hnida told CBS This Morning, "Probably the biggest problem with cracking your knuckles is that it annoys everybody else that you're around." If you are looking for an honest reason to dissuade that knuckle-cracking neighbor, however, one study of people who had regularly cracked their knuckles over a period of 35 years showed that they had slightly swollen joints and a weaker grip than non-knuckle crackers. If you're the one in the habit of cracking your knuckles, doctors recommend doing something else like squeezing on a tennis ball, which will strengthen the muscles instead of weakening them.

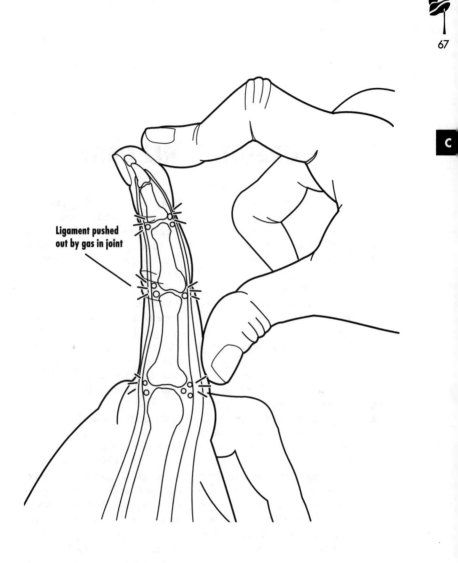

Ligament pushed out by gas in joint

CREDIT CARD DEBT

You pay the minimum balance on your Master Card bill with a handy Discover Card check. You have just enough to make the minimum on your *other* Master Card. You're left with so little cash that you need to use your Visa to buy groceries. Forget it. You will never, ever, ever get out of debt. By that I mean never, not ever. Pigs will fly first.

Make no mistake, the credit card issuers want you to be in debt. They make profits from revolving balances. Since the early 1990s, banks have upped credit limits on their customers' credit cards by more than a third, filling mailboxes with 3 billion offers in 1997. We may complain about ATM fees, but few of us complain about the fees we pay for our plastic.

Studies by economist Lawrence Ausubel of the University of Maryland show that consumers underestimate how much they borrow on their cards. On average, you're carrying more than twice as much debt as you think.

If you carry a credit card balance of $1,750 on a card that charges 18 percent interest and you pay just the minimum and buy nothing more it will take you 22 years and $4,000 in interest to pay it off.

In the early 1980s, U.S. households had 70 cents of debt for every dollar they spent in a year. By 1990, it had risen to 90 cents. Today, according to *American Demographics*, we are carrying almost 99 cents of debt for every dollar we spend.

The only costs we really understand are annual fees and introductory interest rates. Credit card issuers have responded

"OUR LITTLE GOLD MINE" CREDIT CARD

Account Number	Approved Credit Line	Available Credit	Statement Open Date	Close Date	Grace Period	Type of Interest
27891-02-7737-091-666	$10,000	$8,250.00	March 01 - March 31		NO	VARIABLE

Date Posted	Reference Number	Date Purchased	Description of Transaction	Amount
301	98352647690987534 7783	228	GASACO GAS & OIL	$27.52
301	86520784377862765 3478	228	MIKES CAR WASH	$8.95
305	91273789509439809 3203	302	NOVEL BOOKS	$26.89
306	11183264098745637 2821	303	EBAY	$62.38
310	52213907465327982 9047	307	CITY SOCCER YOUTH	$45.00
313	30907876455334258 9854	309	SPORTS OUTLET	$79.53
322	78437786276534788 6520	318	EBAY	$200.15
322	94398093203912737 8950	318	MUNICIPAL UTILITIES	$294.85
322	45533425898543090 70876	318	EVERYWHERE CELLULAR	$39.91
322	74563728211118326 4098	318	EBAY	$69.03
330	52647690987534778 3983	327	EBAY	$280.97
331	27653478865207843 7786	328	STATE BANK/CASH ADVANCE	$250.00

Previous Balance		Payments and Credits	+	Purchases, Fees, and Adjustments	+	FINANCE CHARGE (18.00%)	+	Late Payment Fees	=	New Balance
$364.89		$25.00		$1385.18		$24.93		$0.00		$1750.00

At 18 percent, it takes 22 years to pay this balance off if just paying the minimum

by lowering both. Don't worry, they more than make up for it. Late fees have gone up about 50 percent since 1990. Grace periods have shortened. Some cards penalize you for being one day late.

If you get in trouble, don't expect your creditors to help you out. Once your card is close to its limit and the minimum payment is equal to your monthly paycheck, the issuing bank may raise your interest rates. They can do that if you pay late, exceed your credit limit, or have a deteriorating credit report.

A team of Ohio State University researchers came to the shocking conclusion that all this debt-stress is bad for our health. They conducted two telephone surveys of 1,036 Ohioans and discovered that those who reported higher levels of stress about their debt reported worse health than those with lower levels of debt.

C

CRINKLING CANDY
WRAPPERS AT THE THEATER

See also cell phones, coughing in the theater, laser pointers

You're watching a movie—or trying to. The actors are speaking in hushed voices. "But if we set the fuse.." This is when the guy next to you decides it's time to open a wrapped piece of candy. Crinkle, crackle. "What about the alarm on the..." crinkle, crackle. "The most important thing is..." crinkle, crinkle, crackle, crink. This is when you stand up and shout, "Will you stop that!" A large usher personally escorts you out of the theater.

Whether you're trying to enjoy the show next to a snacking audience member or you're the snacking culprit trying in vain to unwrap a hard candy without attracting attention, those crinkling wrappers are irritating. Fortunately, a pair of scientists has devoted considerable

mental energy to answering the question: "Is there a way to open a plastic wrapper in a theater so that it makes less noise?" Unfortunately, the answer to that question is "no."

It was a fortuitous accident that turned Eric Kramer of Simon's Rock College in Great Barrington, Massachusetts, and Alexander Lobkovsky of the National Institute of Standards and Technology in Gaithersburg, Maryland, into pioneers in the field of annoying candy wrapper research.

They were graduate students at the University of Chicago when they began studying crumpled plastic membranes, hoping their investigations would yield some positive uses in automobile safety, the efficient design of packaging materials, and the properties of two-dimensional polymers.

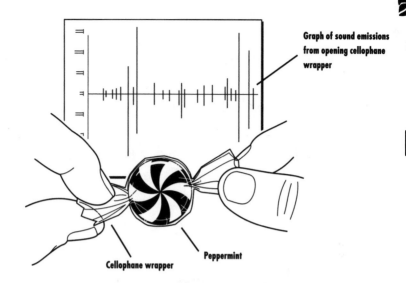

Cellophane wrapper

Peppermint

They began by crumpling a sheet of polyester film 30 to 40 times to make permanent creases. They then made high-resolution digital recordings of the sounds that were produced as they uncreased it. They discovered that the physics of candy wrappers is highly complex. When a flat plastic wrapper is twisted around a piece of candy, it is permanently changed. The creases—the scientists call them disorder in the curvature of the material—are responsible for the noises you hear.

When you think you're just unwrapping a piece of candy, you're actually moving the plastic from one stable configuration to another stable configuration. Every time you do this there is a corresponding click. The sound is not continuous. It is made up of pops that last only a thousandth of a second. The loudness of the random pops has nothing to do with the speed at which you twist the wrapper or even the thickness of the material. In other words, no matter how you do it, it's going to make the same amount of noise.

The best expert advice Kramer and Lobkovsky can give is to open the candy as fast as you can and get it over with.

D

DANDRUFF THROUGH **DUST COATING YOUR COMPUTER**

DANDRUFF

See also dust coating your computer monitor

That little itch could be telling them you have dandruff. Or it could be the fact that your shoulders look like ski slopes, or that you have a bald spot from unremitting clawing at your scalp...

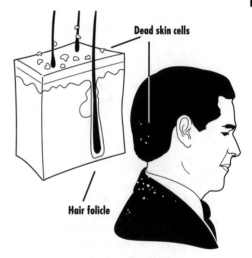

Dead skin cells

Hair follicle

Dandruff is very common—about 50 to 60 million Americans have it. Dermatologists have come to discover that it may be yet another problem caused by an imbalance in the ecosystem of tiny creatures that live on your body. Your scalp is home to a yeast-like organism called Pityrosporum ovale (P. ovale for short). Climate, hormones and other factors can provide a more fertile landscape for P. ovale. Some people's skin over-reacts to the presence of these guys. The immune system kicks in and responds by over-

producing skin cells which are renewed up to 10 times faster than normal. Some scientists, however, think the greater presence of P. ovale is the effect, rather than the cause of the increased skin production.

Whatever the cause, the more skin cells are made, the more

shed. You are always shedding skin, about 400,000 particles a minute, but the skin cells that fall from other parts of your body are so small we only notice them when they accumulate on our computer screens as dust. Your scalp produces more oil than other parts of your body. This binds the skin particles together producing flakes.

The ICR Survey Research Group of Pennsylvania recently questioned 700 people with dandruff. About 21 percent of those surveyed said they'd rather have a headache than dandruff. Another 17 percent would take heartburn over dandruff. Ten percent said they'd be happier during an allergy attack, and 9 percent said they'd gladly exchange it for athlete's foot.

If your dandruff is less pronounced, you are still probably embarrassed about it, thanks to television commercials that tell you you're supposed to be. Half of the survey respondents were self-conscious about it. Men, it turned out, worried more than women—58 percent of the men and 48 percent of the women were as concerned about what other people think as they were about the condition itself.

If you are worried about your wintry shoulders, dandruff shampoos do work. In fact, a recent study showed that over-the-counter dandruff shampoos were as effective as prescription dandruff shampoos. (This is good because it means the over-the-counter stuff is as effective as anything else, but bad because if Head and Shoulders doesn't cure your case of dandruff there's not really anything much better out there.) The main ingredients in dandruff shampoos are zinc pyrithione, selenium sulfide, salicylic acid and coal tars. The active ingredients either retard cell growth (cytostatic) or they loosen and remove cell overgrowth (keratolytic). Some new dandruff shampoos (like Nizirol A-D) employ an antifungal ingredient, ketoconazole, which kills P. ovale.

DENTIST'S DRILL

D

See also aluminum foil against dental fillings, bad breath

Zzzzzzzzzeeeeeeeeeeee. There are few sounds that can put a chill in the spine like the sound of a dentist's drill. The good news is, our children may grow up without ever hearing it. Dental researchers are developing ways to treat cavities that will not involve drills and in a few years, they may even put a stop to the strain of bacteria that causes decay.

Even when your mouth is freshly brushed and clean there are 1,000 to 100,000 bacteria on the surface of each tooth. When you've gone a while between brushings, there can be as many as 1 billion per tooth.

These microorganisms have evolved along with humans. Scientists have discovered that everywhere on earth, even though diets vary, the types of organisms in the mouth remain the same. The bacteria responsible for tooth decay is known as S. mutans. Scientists believe they were once useful to us. Some strains produce natural antibiotics against the bacteria

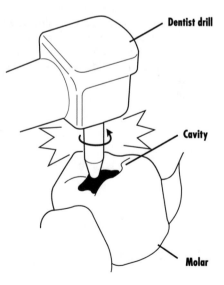

Dentist drill

Cavity

Molar

that cause strep throat. But as we began to eat more refined sugars, things changed. As it eats the sugar, S. mutans produces more acid than the saliva can buffer. The extra acid eats away at the surface of the tooth—that means cavities.

We are not born with our oral ecosystem, but little by little the bacteria, yeast, viruses and protozoa settle in. S. mutans arrives during a "window of infectivity" around the age of two. It comes from dear old mom who leans over and kisses the baby. It doesn't take much saliva to transfer the bacteria. Scientists are now trying to block tooth decay by keeping S. mutans from taking hold during the six-month window of infectivity. Other researchers are experimenting with vaccines that would provide children with antibodies against the bacteria. Still other researchers are developing a harmless strain of S. mutans that might one day replace its acid-producing sibling.

This comes too late for many of us. We spend $20 billion per year treating cavities. Right now the only way to get rid of cavities is by cutting away the decaying portion of the tooth, a procedure that is done almost 170 million times a year.

The dreaded dental drill dates back to the 1700s. Modern high-speed handpieces were introduced in the 1960s. Now new tools are revolutionizing the field. Dentists are using lasers and microabrasion to remove decay without a drill. With any luck, the drill is an annoyance we won't have to live with for long.

D

DIETING

Mmmmm. Celery sticks and Melba toast. Feel full? Of course not! Your 1,200-calorie-a-day diet is leaving you dizzy, sleepless, anxious, short of attention and obsessed with food. You think your hair might be falling out, but you're going to get thin even if it kills you. (There is a small chance that it actually will!)

These days dieting is more common than not dieting. A 1987 study revealed that 95 percent of women have dieted at some time. At this moment, 30 million American women are on diets. Between 95-98 percent of diets fail. By comparison, experimental cancer treatments have a 50 percent chance of success, which led Marilyn Wann, activist and author of *Fat! So?*, to conclude: "You have a better chance of surviving cancer than of losing weight and keeping it off." Yet we keep trying, hoping that we will be one of the successful 2 percent.

"Try as we might to change our shape, most of us will fail," wrote Dean Hamer and Peter Copeland in *Living with Our Genes*. "The reason, scien-

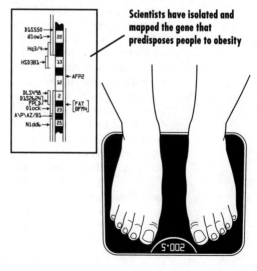

Scientists have isolated and mapped the gene that predisposes people to obesity

tists have learned, is that body weight is more determined by inheritance than by any other factor. Experiments have shown that mice with a certain type of gene grow fat even when they are given almost no food. Humans contain an obese gene that is almost identical to the mouse version, and some people will have a harder time controlling their weight, not because they are weak or eat too much, but because the genetic bar is set higher."

No less an authority than the *New England Journal of Medicine* says that the $30–$50 billion we spend a year on diet products "is wasted." Medical researchers are beginning to believe that the health risks associated with fat may be caused by a sedentary lifestyle rather than the body fat itself. A 1998 study in the *Journal* found no correlation between increasing body weight and decreasing life span. As headlines continually point out, we're facing an "obesity epidemic" in this country, and yet our life spans keep increasing.

"The data linking overweight and death, as well as the data showing the beneficial effects of weight loss are limited, fragmentary, and often ambiguous," wrote the Journal's editors Jerome Kassirer, M.D. and Marcia Angell, M.D. "Many studies fail to consider confounding variables... for example, mortality among overweight people may be misleadingly high because overweight people are more likely to be sedentary and of low socioeconomic status."

There are health risks associated with dieting. One 1991 study showed that the more frequently an individual's weight fluctuated by as little as ten pounds, the more likely that person was to be at risk for cardiac disease. Other studies have linked dieting to gall bladder disease, osteoporosis, depression, anemia, and ironically, weight gain. Yes, dieting makes you fat. It signals your metabolism that you are entering a period of famine. Your body's natural response is to decrease the production of leptin. This sends out a signal to hold on to every calorie that comes in. Repeated bouts of yo-yo dieting tell your body that you're going to face these periods of famine from time to time and it becomes more efficient at storing fat. The dieting you did in the past contributes to your ample behind today.

When it comes to altering your natural shape, there may not be a lot you can do. If your concern is your health, on the other hand, there is good news. Exercise and a diet of nutritious foods (rather than a diet of almost no food) can improve most areas of your health. The Cooper Institute for Aerobics Research studied 30,000 people and found that fat people who are physically active live longer than thin people who sit around most of the time. As Steven Blair, director of research, put it, "If you are a couch potato, being thin provides absolutely no assurance of good health, and does nothing to increase your chances of living a long life." So put on your size 26 leotard and get to the gym! A healthy diet is a balanced diet with lots of fruits and vegetables and not too much fat. Drink plenty of water, get enough sleep and remain physically active. You may lose inches and pounds, or you may not, but you will be healthier.

Oh, and what to do with the $40 billion we spend on diet products? Wann offers the following suggestions: We could fund the National Endowment for the Arts for 250 years, build 2.5 Habitat for Humanity homes for each of the 2.5 million homeless in America, create 66,000 battered women's shelters, pay off the federal deficit twice—or take everyone on earth out to see a movie.

D

DRIPPING FAUCET

Drip. Drip. Drip. Drip. It's water torture. Pure water torture. That is, if you're a woman. You probably have conversations that go like this: "Honey, I thought you said you were going to fix that faucet?" "Yeah. I'm going to get around to it. What's the big deal?" "Isn't that dripping driving you crazy?" "I said I'd get to it. Jeez."

"A dripping faucet falls into a class of aggravating things that is more aggravating to women than to men," says Francis T. McAndrew, professor of psychology at Knox College in Galesburg, Illinois. "They notice them quicker and are bothered by them more. A man is more likely to say 'what noise?'"

The sound of water itself is not irritating. In fact, the sound of a waterfall or a babbling brook is relaxing; but you'll never find a New Age "nature sounds" CD with the title "faucet drip." The faucet, unlike the waterfall, is a sign that something is wrong. It's the constant dripping reminder that something in the home is broken.

"It nags at you because it's not supposed to be there," McAndrew says. "It's a signal that there's something amiss and you can't quite relax and forget about it because there's something that needs to be fixed or water's being wasted or whatever is bothering you."

As to why women are more bothered than men, McAndrew speculates that it has to do with our "hunter-gatherer" roots.

"Women and men are just primed to tune into different things," he says. "There is quite a bit of evidence that women are much better at remembering the location of objects.

The hypothesis is that women were the gatherers so they were better at remembering the locations of things," and presumably to little things that are amiss in the home environment, like that infernal dripping faucet.

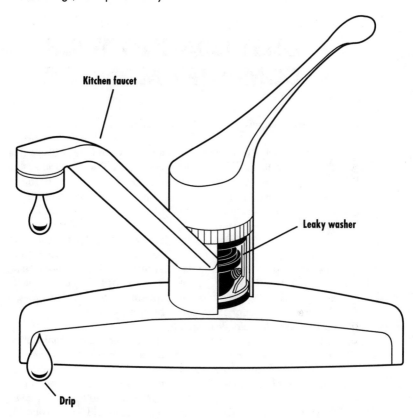

Kitchen faucet

Leaky washer

Drip

D

DUST COATING YOUR COMPUTER MONITOR

See also dandruff

Why is it that no matter how many times you get up and wipe off the screen, you're always running your spreadsheet program through a haze of dust?

Technically, there isn't really such a thing as a "dust molecule." Dust can be just about anything as long as its particles are small enough to be carried through the air—less than 1/10th the width of a human hair. Dust is everywhere. It lands on every surface on just about every part of the planet.

Dr. Joseph Prospero, a professor of atmospheric chemistry at the University of Miami has been studying dust for more than 30 years. His discoveries may give you a new appreciation for the snowy coating on your monitor.

Outdoor dust is made up largely of particles of rock that take to the air as wind and water erode mountains. Prospero found that the red dust that fills the air in many East Coast states comes all the way from Africa. Bermuda's islands would not have top soil were it not for blowing African dust. Some terrestrial dust even comes from outer space, it is deposited into our atmosphere by comets and brought home by gravity.

Indoor dust is a different matter: Some is tracked in from the outside, but most is created in the house. About 40 pounds of dust accumulates in the average household each year. As you may have heard, most of it is made up of your own skin. Human beings shed about 400,000 particles a minute according to chemist and dust expert Armin Clobes.

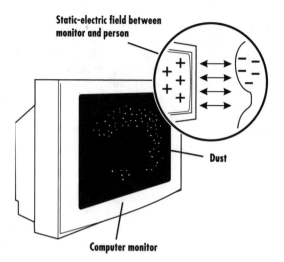

Static-electric field between monitor and person

Dust

Computer monitor

Clobes is a senior research associate for SC Johnson Wax. He uses electron microscopes and lasers to analyze the content of household dust. Our dust is a microscopic version of everything we keep in the home—carpet fibers, food particles, dead bugs, hair, pet dander and clothing lint.

Given the right conditions, dust can even create dust. If there is enough moisture in the air, mold and bacteria grow in piles of dust and create their own dust clouds. All of this is enough to make the housekeeper throw in the towel, but it is important to try to keep household dust at bay. It provides food for dust mites, a distant relative of

the spider. Their waste products can trigger allergic reactions.

Electronics like your computer, television and stereo carry an electric current that generates a field of static energy. Because most dust particles carry an electrical charge, they cling to other charged surfaces. (Sometimes they cling to each other and form dust bunnies.) A dust particle that might just fall off a table sticks to an electronic device because of this attraction.

According to *Electronic Design* magazine, the trajectories of the charged dust particles are influenced by the electric fields between a television or computer monitor and the viewer. Thus, the same coating you see on the screen can be accumulating on your face. When you walk away, however, the electrical field is broken and some of the dust will fall off. And you do wash your face more often than you clean your monitor, don't you?

EARS POPPING THROUGH **ECHO ON THE PHONE LINE**

EARS POPPING IN AIRPLANE

The airplane heads up into the clouds and suddenly you have the sensation of cotton being shoved into your ears—from your skull out. The pilot is giving a safety message, but to you it sounds like the adults in a "Peanuts" cartoon. If you have a cold, you're treated to pain as well.

Fast changes in altitude make your ears feel puffed up and blocked. Scientists have a name for this, they call it barotisis or aerotisis. At ground level, the air pressure in your middle ear is equal to the air pressure that surrounds your head. The higher you go, however, the lower the air pressure becomes. So air flows out of the ear through the eustachian tube and into the nose and throat.

When the plane stops ascending and levels off, your body has a chance to put things back into balance by letting out enough air so your ear pressure matches cabin pressure. Your ears feel fine again until it's time to land. The whole process is reversed as the plane goes down and the air pressure in the cabin increases. Now there is a greater pressure outside than inside your middle ear. The air tries to force its way back into the ear through the eustachian tube. If it has trouble, say you have a head cold that irritates the tiny tube and keeps it shut, you may feel pain.

The best way to keep barotisis at bay on the way up is to equalize ear pressure by swallowing. It opens the eustachian tube and makes it easier for the extra air to escape. This is why people suggest chewing gum. Sipping water or chewing on a snack can serve the same purpose. If that doesn't work, *Prevention* magazine suggests swallowing while holding your nose. This creates a small vacuum that draws pressure from the middle ear.

When you head back down, *Prevention* suggests gently blowing air into your nostrils while holding your nose. This technique has a name—the Valsalva maneuver. It forces air into the middle ear.

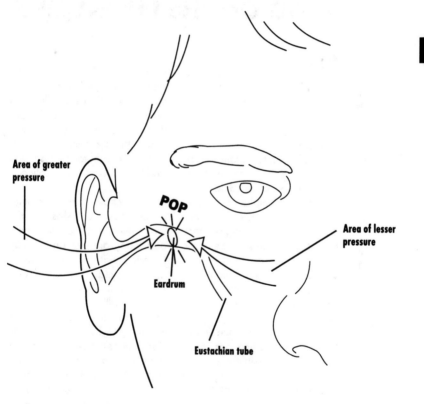

Area of greater pressure

POP

Area of lesser pressure

Eardrum

Eustachian tube

ECHO ON THE PHONE LINE

*"*Hey I...what? Oh sorry... no, you go ahead...Yes, I was...what? No you were talking and...Sorry...There's a delay..."

Little compares to the stops and starts of an international or bi-coastal telephone call that features an echo or delay; but before you complain too much, consider the miracle of technology that is your long-distance call. It takes miles of fiber optic cable and a satellite or two for you to tell grandma about your son's adventures in Little League. That's pretty impressive.

Once the stuff of science fiction, today's communications satellites make it possible to communicate almost instantly anywhere within the line of site of the satellite—about ⅓ of the Earth's surface. Using a network of satellites and cables, virtually the whole world can be reached

by pressing a few numbers. It takes a little less than .3 seconds for a signal carrying your voice to reach the satellite and return to the planet. That means that echoes are heard .6 seconds after the speaker's voice. That's enough to confuse you and trip up your conversation.

Not all echoes come from outer space, however. Most of the major telecommunications channels today are well on the way to being switched over to fiber-optic cabling. A single strand of optical fiber can carry more than 25 trillion bits per second of information. Some of the major lines have as many as 288 strands of fiber—that means there is a lot of room for your signal. Switching to fiber optic cable is expensive, however, and the lines that connect your house or office to the "back-bone trunks" are probably not made of the stuff. Telecommunications types call this the "last mile problem."

As a result, the signal coming from your home must be converted in the telephone company's central office switch before it goes out over the long-distance lines. This causes a brief delay, which you perceive as an echo. It doesn't have to be much of a delay, 30 milliseconds is perceptible and 50 is downright irritating.

Finally there is something called "acoustic echo." Most common on speaker phones and small cell phones, acoustic echo is feedback caused by the sound from the speaker being picked up by the receiver. Hands-free car phones are especially prone to this type of acoustic echo. When you talk inside a car, your voice is reflected off the various surfaces and all those echoes return to the hand piece at various times.

Telephone companies and manufacturers of telephones, modems and wireless communications devices are working to combat the problems with echo cancellation technology, which promises to put an end to... I'm sorry, were you saying something?

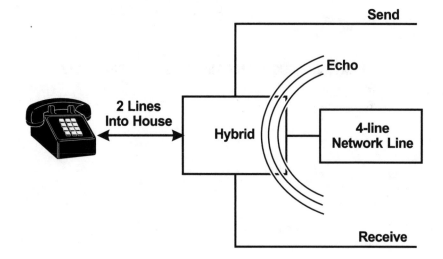

FARTS THROUGH **FREE TIME? WHAT FREE TIME?**

F

FARTS

You digest, you create gas. Simple as that. Everyone does it—an average of 10 times a day. Certain foods are infamous for their gas-producing ability. Beans, broccoli, cabbage and apples contain complex sugars that can't be broken down by digestive juices. Bacteria in the intestines ferment them and the result is gas. You'll be pleased to know that scientists have devoted a great deal of mental energy to the study of farts. In 1967, for example, the New York Academy of Sciences held an entire two day conference on the subject of gastrointestinal gas. A pair of Australians, gastroenterologist Terry Bolin and nutritionist Rosemary Stanton, wrote a book, *Wind Breaks,* on the subject. It is now in its third printing.

The top researcher today is probably Dr. Michael Levitt, chief of research at the Minneapolis Veterans Administration Hospital, who has been studying our emissions since 1965. He has learned that some people pass gas more often and others pass larger volumes less often, but the total volume remains roughly the same, up to

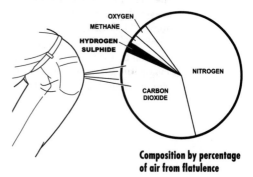

Composition by percentage of air from flatulence

2,000 milliliters, or about 120 cubic inches of gas a day. Frequency depends on the sensitivity of the walls of the rectum. The more sensitive it is to distension the more frequently it will release the emissions. With age, the bowel becomes less elastic and more sensitive to being distended, thus older people fart more frequently, but continue to have the same overall output of gas.

Most of it is odorless. Only 1 part in 10,000 is stinky. It is primarily made up of nitrogen, oxygen, carbon dioxide, hydrogen and methane. The first two ingredients are swallowed while eating. When you belch it is mostly made up of these swallowed gases so it doesn't smell as bad as the stuff that comes out the other end.

The rest of the ingredients in intestinal gas are produced in house. Half of it comes from what we eat. The rest comes from our bile, and the mucus and linings of the intestines. Levitt and his team dressed volunteers in gas-tight Mylar pants and collected their gaseous output then filtered it until the subjects reported it no longer smelled bad. They learned that the distinctive smell comes from hydrogen sulfide, methanethiol and dimethyl sulfide. Sulfur is the key ingredient in all of them.

If you've ever described a particularly nasty fart as "lethal" you were not that far off. The gases are similar chemically to the odorant added to natural gas so we can detect leaks. The brain apparently has the same thing in mind when it reacts to the fragrance. The sulfur-based gases are highly toxic, Levitt says, so we have evolved to detect them at very low levels. The brain perceives of the scent as offensive so we try to get away from it. Don't have to tell me twice.

FINGERNAILS ON A BLACKBOARD

See also annoying music, booming car stereos, car alarms, noise.

The world is full of annoying sounds—crying babies, car horns, Rosanne's singing—but the king of them all has to be the sound of fingernails on a blackboard. It is so universally despised it has become a metaphor for awful noise and anything that frays the nerves. What makes the high-pitched scrape so difficult to hear? Believe it or not, scientists have devoted a fair amount of attention, energy and resources to this perplexing question, but they have yet to come to a consensus.

Researchers Lynn Halpern, Randy Blake and Jim Hillenbrand of Northwestern University investigated the "psyhoacoustics of a chilling sound" by having 24 adult volunteers listen to noises and report their reactions. As expected, the subjects almost all cringed at the blackboard sound. The research team suspected that it was the high-pitched portion of the sound that made listeners shiver. They filtered it out and played the remaining sound to

F

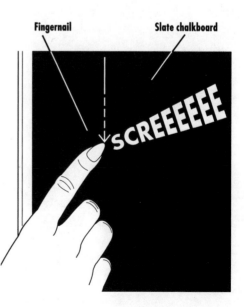

Fingernail   Slate chalkboard

SCREEEEEE

their subjects. To the researchers' surprise, they discovered that the volunteers still found the sound unpleasant. Interestingly, when they removed the lower pitched portion of the sound, the volunteers didn't mind it.

William Yost, president of the Parmly Hearing Institute at Loyola University speculates that the reason people found the second recording bearable was that they no longer recognized it as fingernails on a blackboard and that it is the image of actually running one's fingernails down the slate surface of a blackboard that creates the discomfort, not the sound itself.

The Northwestern team has its own theory. They compared the wave forms of fingernails on a blackboard with those of the warning cries of macaque monkeys. They found there was a strong resemblance. Randy Blake wrote in *Psychology Today*, "We speculate that our spine-tingling aversion to sounds like fingernails scraped over a surface may be a vestigial reflex."

FLAT BEER

It was so refreshing, that first sip of frothy, cold beer on a summer afternoon. Now it's warm and bitter with nothing but a little white circle on top where the foam used to be.

Beer is fizzy because of carbon dioxide, which is generated either by the action of yeasts and sugars in the drink or added at the brewery. In a can, bottle or keg, the CO_2 is kept inside because of the pressure of the container. When the container is opened, the pressure drops and gas escapes.

If you pour your beer into a glass, or if it is contained in a sufficiently clear bottle, you will see tiny bubbles rising to the top in streams along the inside of the glass surface. The bubbles seem to emanate from invisible points. Even though the glass appears to be smooth, the surface has tiny nicks and crev-

ices in it. These hold air pockets, which attract molecules of carbon dioxide. Carbon dioxide is attracted to both the liquid and the air pocket, so it is suspended there for a time. Finally, the air pocket wins out

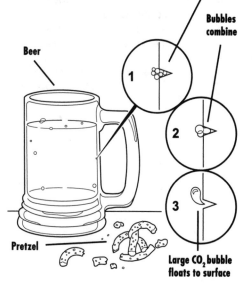

Microscopic CO_2 bubbles collect in nick in glass

Bubbles combine

Beer

1

2

3

Pretzel

Large CO_2 bubble floats to surface

and CO_2 molecules cling together along the surface of the crevice. Once the bubble becomes too buoyant to be held down, it breaks away and rises to the surface and a new bubble starts to form.

At the top of the liquid, the bubbles form foam—the head on a mug of beer. Eventually, the bubbles burst and the head collapses. The bubbles burst faster if they come into contact with fat. Lipstick and the oil on your skin can thus deflate the froth.

Cold liquids can hold more carbonation than warm liquids, so as your beer warms up, its ability to hold CO_2 decreases. More of the gas escapes to the surface and dissipates. Eventually there are no bubbles left.

A team of British researchers from the Institute of Food Research (IFR) in Norwich and Brewing Research International in Surrey have taken on the vital task of beer-head preservation. The scientists are studying some of the proteins in barley (an ingredient in beer) that protect the plant from attack by pathogens. "It was something of a surprise to discover that they might also prove very useful in counteracting the effects of crisp-eating on beer foam," an IFR press release said.

They discovered that some of these proteins contain a pocket which can "mop up" fat molecules and keep them from bursting the foam bubbles in beer. Once they figure out exactly how the process works, they hope to be able to make recommendations on brewing methods to keep you in suds.

FLEAS

See also ants, cockroaches, flies, gnats, mosquitoes

F

Fido's foes are all over your house. The dog is scratching its fur off. You can't walk through the carpet without little insects jumping at your heels. Need any more reason to hate fleas? How about this—their mass murdering ancestors killed off a fourth of Europe's population by spreading the bubonic plague during the Middle Ages.

There are about 1,600 species of fleas in the world. The medical entomologist John W. Maunder once said he has evidence of a "vast flea epidemic" throughout Western Europe and much of the U.S. In all, the world's fleas probably weigh more than the world's humans. From 1991–1992, the requests for flea extermination increased by over 70 percent. If your cat has fleas, there may be only a

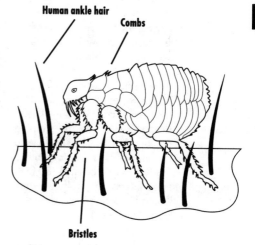

Human ankle hair

Combs

Bristles

dozen or two on the animal. Another 10,000 may be hiding out in the carpet waiting for a warm-blooded host to walk by.

All are tiny, wingless insects with a taste for blood. Their bodies are fortified with a row of spines above their mouthparts (on their back). These are called the combs or ctenidia. Entomologists used to believe these helped the fleas move through fur or feathers. Now they believe the setae, bristles on the legs, help them move while the combs make it difficult for you to pluck them out of your pet's fur. If you've ever tried to do this, you've seen firsthand how effective they are. Fleas' hard, pointy heads are perfect for burrowing, and their mouthparts allow them to pierce skin and suck blood.

They measure between .04 to .4 inches in length. Don't let their diminutive size fool you—they're strong. If you had the jumping ability of the flea, you could leap to the top of a 25-story building in a single bound—30,000 times in row. (Men: If you were "hung like a flea," you'd have a pair of penises.)

Some fleas are picky eaters, preferring the blood of only one species, but others will snack on another creature if their preferred host is unavailable—cat fleas fall into this category. Fluffy's fleas will bite you in a pinch. The most popular mammals, though, are rodents. Fleas love rats. They're not nearly as fond of horses, monkeys, apes and humans.

Flea's eggs are the size of a pinhead. If your pet is infested, you can probably see them in the fur. They look like specks of dirt. When they hatch, mom and dad feed the larvae with their blood-rich feces (Yum!). If their parent's droppings aren't available, they eat one another. The larva make cocoons and, depending on the species, they stay there for a few days or months. Then they emerge as fully grown adults ready to suck some blood.

No fleas in your home? You can go look at them in a museum. The largest flea collection in the world is housed in the British Museum in London. There are also collections at the Canadian National Museum in Ottawa and at the Smithsonian in Washington D.C.

FLIES

See also ants, cockroaches, fleas, gnats, mosquitoes

It buzzes around your ear, taunting you. It knows you won't get it with that swatter. You swat, swat, swat and it just laughs at you with that little fly bzzzzz. The reason the fly always seems to get away is that its compound eyes give the insect the ability to respond to light 10 times faster than we can. It sees that swatter coming and flies away with wings that beat about 180 times a second (that's also what causes the buzzing sound). Are you ready to give up and move to Alaska? Forget it—the common house-fly, *Musca domestica*, flies EVERYWHERE there are human beings. They're in Alaska and in the deserts. One trash can may serve as a breeding ground for more than 30,000 maggots a week. (Nope, they're not even cute as babies.)

Depending on which expert you ask, there are between 120,000 and more than a million different kinds of flies in the world. They can walk upside down on ceilings with glands on their feet that produce a sticky substance.

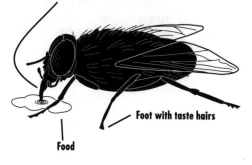

Upchuck of digestive enzymes to liquify food

Foot with taste hairs

Food

Flies can also taste with those feet. They have 1,500 taste hairs, which can savor the flavor of a sugar cube or a cow patty, two fly favorites. To be fair, flies don't actually eat dung. That would be gross. They drink the moisture from it. This is because flies urinate every few minutes and they need to replenish the liquid regularly.

Adult flies can't chew. They sponge up food. That means they have to convert whatever they eat into liquid. They do this by throwing up. Put another way, they expel digestive enzymes onto food to start breaking it down before they eat it. Then, with the help of a pumping organ in the head, they suck up the liquid using a spongelike mouth part. If you're not sufficiently irritated by flies now, here's yet another reason to dislike them: Flies have been known to carry such diseases as typhoid fever, cholera, dysentery, trachoma and anthrax, which they spread with their unique feeding habits.

There is one piece of good news about flies. Baby flies—that is maggots—have medical uses. As creepy as the idea may seem, many doctors are using the larvae to eat away dead infected tissue from wounds. They eat the infected tissue while sparing healthy tissue. There is also evidence that the maggots exude antibacterial chemicals such as allantoin. Physicians put a quantity of maggots—from a dozen to a hundred or so—into an infected wound and keep them in place with a dressing designed to protect intact skin from the potent enzymes produced by the maggots. An average dose of larvae can digest around 14 grams of dead tissue a day. Yum.

FOOT'S ASLEEP AND FOOT CRAMP

You've been sitting for a while when... pins and needles... pins and needles in your foot. If your foot is asleep, it must be having nightmares. Feet do not "fall asleep" because the circulation has been cut off. If your circulation is interrupted the result is a leg cramp. A foot falling asleep is irritating. A leg cramp is painful. What happens during a cramp is that a calf or foot muscle goes into spasm and shuts down the blood flow, depriving muscles of oxygen.

A sleeping foot has nothing to do with your veins. A foot usually falls asleep when you've been sitting cross-legged. The peroneal nerve, which runs through the knee and sends messages from the foot to the brain, becomes compressed. As a result, your brain gets all kinds of screwy messages about the "foot," which is actually perfectly fine. People often stand and stomp their feet trying to "restore circulation." It does work, but not for the reasons they think. By standing you stretch the nerve back to its normal shape and the odd signals stop.

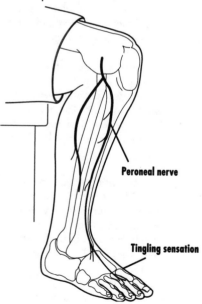

Peroneal nerve

Tingling sensation

FREE TIME?
WHAT FREE TIME?

See also caught in traffic, credit card debt, office cubicles, TV always on

I can't talk now I have to pick up the kids and take them to band practice and cook dinner and work on my report for tomorrow's annual meeting and mend my jacket and learn French.

As late as the 1980s, forecasters were predicting that by 2000 our biggest problem would be what to do with the almost unlimited leisure time technology would grant us. By 1999 the tune had changed. That year, an issue of *American Demographics* magazine predicted that: "The cry of the needy in the new millennium may well be 'Brother, can you spare some time?' Harried baby boomers will create a time famine for themselves by working more hours and committing to more family and community obliga-tions. Marjorie Valin of the Washington, D.C.–based American Advertising Federation says advertisers of the future will need to capitalize on what she calls 'the frenetic sense of lost time' and the life-out-of-control angst that permeates modern culture. "

Some experts believe we're not actually any more pressed for time than previous generations, we just believe we are. Time-use experts John P. Robinson and Geoffrey Godbey's book *Time For Life* asserts that Americans have almost five hours more free time per week than in the 1960s. In fact, we average about 40 hours of free time per week (away from work, meals, housekeeping chores, child care and sleep). That is a gain of almost one hour per day since 1965. Yet most estimate they have about 16 hours a week of free time.

To Do List

Pick up dry cleaning

Get Bob's birthday gift!

groceries

Fido-clipping 10:30

doc appt 2:00

Write report ASAP!

mow the lawn

As people feel more stressed, they tend to misreport the length of time at work to a greater degree. They use "lack of time" as a shorthand for feeling stressed. Godbey believes we feel more rushed because 25 of our 40 hours of leisure time fall on weekdays and come in chunks of an hour or two, he claims. "In many cases, that time does not provide for psychological release. If leisure means tranquility, these hour-long chunks may not have much effect."

Another reason for our obsession with time is that as our roles in society become less rigid, more and more of our position in life is determined by portable skills and credentials. Therefore, to increase our value in our chosen careers and society, we need to have chalked up many measurable accomplishments. We want to already have done these things. We have more goals—too many goals—and we burn ourselves out trying to accomplish them. It's not actually the amount of time that gets us, but the number of things we have to keep track of in our minds. When people in labs are asked to do too many things at once, they show increased tension, diminished perceived control and physical discomfort.

Some historians, however, question whether we really even feel more time pressure than our ancestors. Maybe we just believe we do. They point out that more than 150 years ago, Alexis de Tocqueville, the French commentator on life in the colonies, observed that Americans were always in a hurry.

"It is an age of nervousness... the growing malady of the day, the physiological feature of the age," said a *New York Tribune* editorial. "Nowhere are the rush and hurry and overstrain of life more marked than in this much-achieving Nation... Inventions, discoveries, achievements of science all add to the sum of that which is to be learned, and widen the field in which there is work to be done. If knowledge has increased, we should take more time for acquiring it... For it would be a sorry ending of this splendid age of learning and of labor to be known as an age of unsettled brains and shattered nerves." The article was written in 1895.

GNATS THROUGH **GNATS**

GNATS

See also ants, cockroaches, fleas, flies, mosquitoes

Gnats are the kind of insects for which the word "pest" was invented. Even the Columbia Encyclopedia has officially dubbed them "irritating." The word "gnat" actually describes a variety of small, two-winged insects. They're most infamous for their habit of swarming around people's faces on warm summer days. From the gnat's perspective, the swarm is something akin to a singles bar. As part of their mating ritual, males gather en masse around a recognizable object—a bush, a pole or a person standing in a parking lot. There they wait for their female counterparts. They are short lived and only have a few weeks to pass on their genetic code so they are persistent. Flies, incidentally, congregate around dung for a similar reason. Animal waste is full of bacteria that baby flies (maggots) eat. It is also full of moisture that the adults can drink. Thus, male and female flies meet and mate near dung because it's the perfect spot to lay their eggs.

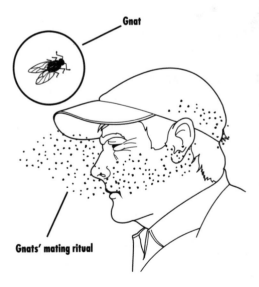

Gnat

Gnats' mating ritual

HANGNAILS THROUGH **HITTING THE FUNNY BONE**

HANGNAILS

See also paper cuts

They aren't nails and they don't hang. A hangnail is actually a split cuticle. The little bit of jutting skin can peel away from the finger leaving the red, raw skin underneath exposed. They hurt. That's how they got their name. It comes from the Anglo-Saxon *ang* meaning 'painful' and *naegl* meaning 'nail'. Thus, a pain near the nail. Where the "H" came from is anyone's guess.

The cuticle splits because the skin gets too dry or, on occasion, because of a bad manicure. People may joke about someone crying over a hangnail, but they are much more painful than it seems they should be. Your fingertips are a sense organ—they are the part you most frequently use to reach out and touch something. Therefore, they are full of sensitive nerve endings as well as tiny blood vessels. When you're injured there, the nerves fire like mad. What is more, a hangnail can cause something more serious—paronychia, one of the most common hand infections. If a germ known as Staphylococcus aureus gets into the torn skin, it can cause an infection with swelling, tenderness and more pain. As tempted as you may be to peel away that little bit of skin, don't. You're likely to tear the skin even more and open it up to a number of nasty organisms.

Instead, soak hangnails in warm water for about 10 minutes twice a day. Use manicure scissors to trim off any sharp, dried skin around the edge of the nail. Then rub petroleum jelly over and around the nail and leave it on overnight. The goo will trap moisture and soften the dry skin underneath.

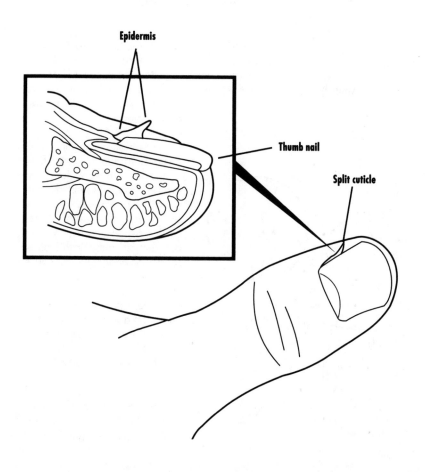

Epidermis

Thumb nail

Split cuticle

HEMORRHOIDS, OR THANKS, I THINK I'LL STAND

Hemorrhoids, also known as piles or "haemorrhoids" if you're British, occur when the small anorectal veins (the ones that surround the rectum and anus) become enlarged and swollen. In other words, if you have hemorrhoids, you have varicose veins in rather embarrassing places.

The word comes from the Greek *hemorrhoia* meaning 'a flow of blood'. The way the word evolved suggests that hemorrhoids have haunted humanity since the early days of recorded history. As Dr. William S. Haubrich put it in his book *Medical Meanings*, "because the condition was frequent, the source of the bleeding was referred to, anatomically, as 'the hemorrhoidal veins.' In other words, the bleeding was named first and then the name was transferred to the source."

There are two major types of hemorrhoids—external and internal. As the name suggests, external hemorrhoids happen

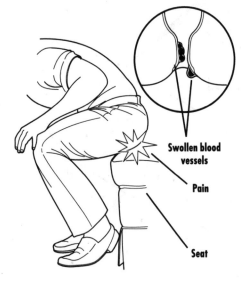

Swollen blood vessels

Pain

Seat

outside the opening of the anus. Internal hemorrhoids are found inside the rectum. The external kind are actually more painful because there is a larger nerve supply there.

Hemorrhoids are caused by pressure in the abdomen, which transmits pressure to the ano-rectal veins. Sitting for long periods of time can supply this kind of pressure. So can straining bowel movements when you're constipated.

Hemorrhoids are common during pregnancy because of the pressure placed on the veins by the enlarged womb. Furthermore, the hormones released during pregnancy tend to relax the supporting muscles, exacerbating the problem. Meanwhile, a woman's blood supply increases during pregnancy, thus raising the pressure within her veins. Not only that, constipation is fairly common during pregnancy.

Medical Update recommends against using over the counter ointments to treat hemorrhoids. Many relied on "live yeast cell derivatives" as their active ingredients. The FDA banned these ingredients as ineffective in 1994, but the products, like Preparation H, reworked their formulas with other approved ingredients. According to the journal, these ingredients do not necessarily do anything for hemorrhoids. The best thing to do is to avoid constipation by getting enough dietary fiber and keep the area clean with baby wipes or witch hazel. To relieve the pain, you may also try a sitz bath. Sit for several minutes in a few inches of water that's as hot as you can handle. It helps improve circulation. Recent studies have demonstrated that the application of nitroglycerine cream, which is commonly used for angina in heart patients, may be beneficial in relieving the pain of swollen hemorrhoids. Just don't sit down too fast.

HERNIA EXAMS

See also medical gibberish

Is it really necessary to "turn your head and cough," or does the doctor just say that to distract you from what he's doing down there? The word hernia comes from the Greek, hernos meaning 'sprout'. It was so named because the unsightly bulge of a hernia resembled the bud of a plant. In inguinal hernias, the kind your doctor is checking for, protruding tissue

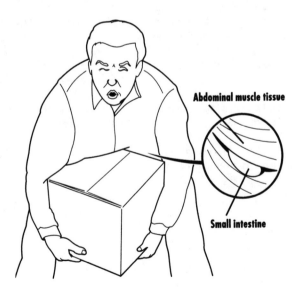

Abdominal muscle tissue

Small intestine

descends along the canal that holds the spermatic cord. Some children are born with small gaps in the abdominal tissue. Other people acquire them through overexertion as in jumping, lifting heavy weight or violent coughing. Women can also get hernias, but they are more frequent among men because of their greater physical exertions and because the canal for the spermatic cord leading through the abdominal wall is wider than the canal for the round ligament in women.

Sometimes hernias can become so large that loops of the intestine can slide through, but smaller hernias pose a greater danger because a loop of the bowel can become pinched and obstructed. Small hernias are often not detected by the patient. For the doctor to be able to feel a gap, he needs to get the patient to increase the pressure in the abdomen and cause the hernia sac to bulge outward. Coughing does the trick. It causes the abdominal muscles to contract and creates the needed pressure. Why do you have to turn your head? The doctor doesn't want you coughing in his face. The good news is that most patients only have to put up with the test once a year. Next time you get into a debate about the worst possible jobs, however, you might win by mentioning surrogate patients. Many medical schools now offer genital-teaching associate programs to show students how to make patients more comfortable during the less modest exams. Surrogate patients can undergo 10-20 prostate, hernia, rectal, breast or pelvic exams by medical students in a single day. The University of South Florida pays the subjects $37.50 an hour, in case you wanted to apply.

H

H

HICCUPS

Everyone is—hic—laughing at your pred-HIC-a-ment, but hic, hic, hiccups hurt. Your friends are running up behind you shouting- BOO! But you're, hic, not cured. Hic! They're making you jump up and down on one leg and drink from the other side of the glass. Now you look stupid and you're covered in water but HIC!

Hiccups have been part of the medical literature since Hippocrates' time. In all those years, physicians haven't quite figured out what makes them happen. They don't help in digestion or anything else that doctors can recognize. They can explain the mechanics of hiccups, however. Hiccups are caused by spasms of the diaphragm. When the muscle's movements get out of rhythm you take in big gulps of air. As your lungs quickly fill, your brain tries to put a stop to it by closing the throat. The vocal cords snap shut. The rush of air creates the "hic" sound.

There hasn't been much serious study of hiccups because the phenomenon is usually very brief. One of the nation's few hiccup experts, Dr. Paul Rousseau of the Carl T. Hayden

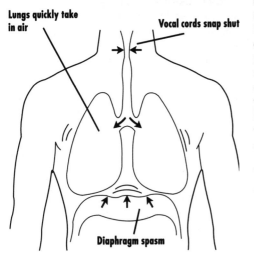

Lungs quickly take in air

Vocal cords snap shut

Diaphragm spasm

VA Medical Center in Phoenix, says that hiccups can occur in spurts of fewer than 7 or more than 63. They generally hit at a rate of 4 to 60 a minute.

In extreme cases, hiccupping is more than a nuisance. Some victims of chronic persistent hiccups have suffered for decades. They have trouble holding conversations or eating anything that takes time to chew. The world record holder in hiccups, according to *Guinness World Records 2000,* is Charles Osborne of Anthon, Iowa, who hiccupped from 1922 until February 1990. Rousseau came across a few cases of death by hiccup in his research. In 2000, the *Washington Times* reported that two Washington, D.C., residents were fitted with pacemakers, which delivered electrical impulses to the phrenic nerves in an effort to end years of uncontrolled hic-ing.

According to Dr. S. Gregory Hipskind, you can cure hiccups by rubbing an ice cube on your neck right around the Adam's apple. Apparently this blocks the nerve impulses that cause the diaphragm to spasm. There is some science behind some of those home remedies. Breathing into a paper bag forces a hiccupper to breathe in more carbon dioxide which helps regulate breathing. Sipping water from the opposite side of the glass stretches the neck and stimulates the vagal nerve in the brain that helps in swallowing the breathing.

If you're looking for a more controversial hiccup cure—a researcher writing in the medical journal the *Lancet* in 1999 reported that marijuana might help cure a stubborn case of the hiccups. After hiccupping for nine days, a patient smoked a joint and the spasms stopped. "Honest officer, hic, I am using marijuana for medical reasons, hic."

H

HITTING THE FUNNY BONE: IT'S NOT FUNNY!

It hurts when you hit the "funny bone." It's not funny at all. Not only that, it's not a bone. It's a vulnerable nerve. The ulnar nerve passes behind the humerus in the cubital tunnel, a bony passageway. The nerve controls muscles used for gripping, pinching and fine movement. It's in charge of signaling most of the muscles in your hand with the exception of the two muscles that lift the thumb up.

A lot of sensory information passes along the ulnar nerve between these muscles and the brain. If you hit your arm just there, your brain gets overloaded with signals. You get that "amusing" tingling, pricking sensation down the whole length of the nerve to the side of the hand, followed by numbness.

Here's the "funny" part of the story: Clever 19th-century doctors saw the connection between the odd sensation of hitting your ulnar nerve and the "humerus" and they decided the whole thing was "humorous" or "funny." Thus, funny bone. In the good old days, some Americans dubbed it "the crazy bone."

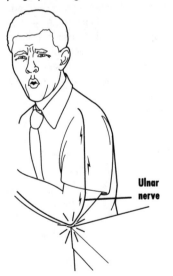

Ulnar nerve

I

ICE CREAM HEADACHE THROUGH **INTERRUPTING**

ICE CREAM HEADACHE OR "BRAIN FREEZE"

What is the most common cause of headaches? Stress? Hangovers? Poor posture? According to Joseph Hulihan of Temple University, it is ice cream. He published his findings in the *British Medical Journal* in 1997.

Whether or not you've ever had a migraine, chances are you've experienced the sensation of indulging in a mouthful of Ben and Jerry's only to be rewarded with a sharp pain in the temple. Medical researchers have a name for ice cream headache: They call it "ice cream headache."

In 1998, Americans spent $11 billion on frozen deserts and consumed 1.3 billion gallons of them. Studies show one out of three Americans have experienced the 30–60 second shooting pain of brain freeze.

The cause is still a mystery, but you'll be pleased to know that scholars throughout the world are working on the problem. One of the earliest brain-freeze researchers was R.O. Smith who, in 1968, experimented on himself by moving crushed ice around in his mouth. He learned it was the back of the soft palate that was sensitive to the temperature change.

The researchers disagree on why this gives you a headache. Some theorize the pain is caused by the rapid cooling of air in the sinuses. Thomas N. Ward of the American Council for Headache Education (ACHE—honest) believes ice cold Cherry Garcia has an effect on the trigeminal nerve, associated with migraines. Merle Diamond of Chicago's Diamond Headache Clinic blames the glossopharyngeal nerve. Some studies say you're more likely to experience ice cream headache if you suffer from migraines, other studies reveal the opposite.

J. W. Sleigh, a senior lecturer at Waikato Hospital in Hamilton, New Zealand, followed up on Hulihan's report by conducting his own study using transcranial Doppler ultrasonography. He measured the speed of cerebral blood flow of three people as they ate ice cream. Two got ice cream headache, one did not. He found that blood flow decreased in the headache sufferers. "Although the brain temperature was not directly measured," he concluded, "these observations suggest that cerebral vasoconstriction causing a decrease in flow may be important in the development of an ice cream headache."

Research continues. Meanwhile, you can avoid the pain by warming the ice cream in the front of your mouth or putting your tongue against your soft palate to heat it up.

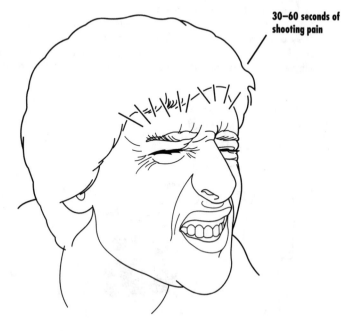

30–60 seconds of shooting pain

IMPROVEMENTS THAT MAKE THINGS WORSE

See also cell phones, computers, internet flaming, laser pointers, powerpointization of the nation

"For the ways in which technology has not improved the quality of life press one." They are designed to make life simpler, to make business more efficient, to put an end to extraneous work. Yet nearly everyone has had an experience with a new machine that stops all work in an office for weeks and then slows it down for months while everyone learns it.

Edward Tenner, executive science and history editor of Prince-ton University Press, calls such things "revenge effects."

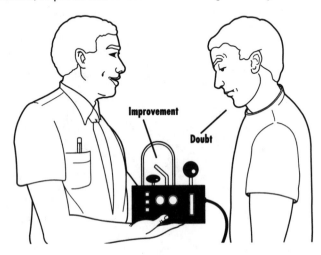

Improvement

Doubt

His book *Why Things Bite Back: Technology and the Revenge of Unintended Consequences* argues that our failure to see things as they operate within systems often leads to unforeseen negative results.

The increasing speed of our modes of transportation has had the revenge effect of rapidly increasing the infestation of parasites, rodents and viruses around the world. Our plush wall to wall carpets have had the revenge effect of dust mites and allergens. "Labor saving" appliances, like vacuum cleaners can create more work. It is less work to vacuum than to beat a rug, but because we have a vacuum, we feel we must clean more often.

Doctors wear surgical gloves to protect patients from germs, but according to the *European Journal of Surgery,* the powder applied to the gloves may cause inflammation, which increases the risk for infection as well as causing false cancer and HIV di-agnoses. Many household products designed to make the living environment cleaner and healthier fill the air with potentially toxic chemicals. New software can have revenge effects of confusion and data loss.

"A machine can't appear to have a will of its own unless it is a system, not just a device," Tenner writes. "It needs parts that interact in unexpected and sometimes unstable and unwanted ways."

The Germans, always economical with language, have a single word for revenge effects—*schlimmbesserung,* literally 'worse betterment'. Related is the Yiddish word *farpotshket.* If you have ever started out with a minor software glitch and, in the course of trying to correct it, wound up completely unable to start your operating system, you have a farpotshket computer. The adjective refers to something that is all fouled up, especially through repeated failed efforts to fix it.

INEFFICIENT SIDEWALK PASS AKA THE SIDEWALK DANCE

See also armrest wars, office cubicles, standing too close

You're walking down the street. A stranger is coming towards you. You dodge to the left to get out of the way, but he dodges to the left too. So you correct to the right, just as he corrects to the right. You shift left again, and he shifts left. You continue with this awkward little dance until you both plant your feet and verbally negotiate passage.

This little episode plays itself out more frequently in the lives of men than women, but we've all done the sidewalk dance at some time. We don't talk about it, but passing on the sidewalk is a complex social interaction with a set of rules and regulations. You'll never get a ticket for making an illegal pass on the sidewalk, but if you stray from the rules you will have some awkward moments or a collision.

In the U.S. and Canada, you are expected to acknowledge someone on the street with eye contact when you are about eight feet apart. If you spot someone you know coming your way from a distance, you look down and pretend not to see them. If you acknowledge him too soon, you're faced with the embarrassment of having to continue to recognize him for the entire length of a corridor. You must then make all kinds of smiles, gestures and dopey expressions of recognition until you get up to the person to say "hello." By that time, you're both feeling so silly that you don't want to be recognized.

When passing a stranger, you communicate your intentions nonverbally at the eight-foot mark. You make eye contact, then look at the path where you intend to walk. The other person is supposed to pick up on this and move the other way. If you miss the glance, both glance at once, or you don't communicate your intentions in time, you end up miscorrecting. Men collide more frequently than women because studies have shown two men pass at a closer distance than two women or a man and a woman. Some scholars believe men crash more often because they both refuse to yield to the other's wishes.

"Some people have tried to make hay out of this by talking about it as a dominance display, like a game of chicken," says Francis T. McAndrew, professor of psychology at Knox College and author of the book *Environmental Psychology.* "I'm told that in some countries, Mexico comes to mind as one, there's actually sort of a game that men play on the street. They pretend they don't see the

other guy and wait for him to move first. If nobody moves and they crash into each other, it doesn't lead to any violence. There are the profuse apologies and everyone goes on their way, but nonetheless, it's sort of oneupmanship about who has to move first."

If you get into a sidewalk dance, avoiding eye contact can sometimes help. So does loudly announcing, "I am moving to the right!"

Eye contact

Collision course

INTERNET FLAMING

See also computer viruses, computers, improvements that make things worse, unsolicited bulk e-mail

"Learn how to spell the word bulletin board before you post on the @#$% board you @#$% idiot. I get so fed up with morons like you wasting everybody's time. Why don't you @#%$ and give your keyboard to someone with opposable thumbs."

If you spend any time at all in Internet chat rooms or discussion forums, you have probably been confronted with a response like this—angry, per-

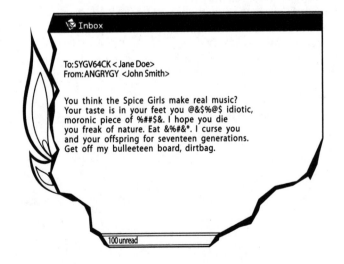

📧 Inbox

To: SYGV64CK < Jane Doe>
From: ANGRYGY <John Smith>

You think the Spice Girls make real music?
Your taste is in your feet you @&$%@$ idiotic,
moronic piece of %##$&. I hope you die
you freak of nature. Eat &%#&*. I curse you
and your offspring for seventeen generations.
Get off my bulleeteen board, dirtbag.

100 unread

sonal, rude and entirely out of proportion to your supposed crime. Grammatical errors, asking something that is in the Frequently Asked Questions, even off-hand comments you think are innocuous can elicit a string of invectives, given the right personalities and circumstances. Why is it that people who are basically kind and polite in normal life are so quick to attack on-line?

As with many human interactions, the reasons are many and complex. When John Q. Netuser gets to his favorite discussion forum, his computing experience may already have put him in a bad mood. There are the delays in getting logged in, the busy signals, disconnects, Internet slowdowns and web pages that have so many Java applets and singing, dancing graphics that they take forever to load. His e-mail box may contain nothing but junk e-mail and a message or two flaming him.

Psychological research confirms what we already know. People don't always behave rationally when they're in a bad mood. Psychologists call this a "state of negative affect." John, in his negative affect, is more likely

to see everything around him in the most negative terms.

Using his screen name 248504325@Compuserve.com, John feels fairly anonymous. He feels free from the kinds of repercussions he'd feel speaking to someone face to face. Even if he alienates everyone, he knows he can always quit the group or get a new screen name and start over. That said, he is actually more concerned about how others view him than he will admit.

John Q. Netuser spends his free time in the "Music of the 80s" forums where he has free reign to show off the knowledge he gained during his many years of MTV viewing. He enters the forum, in his foul mood, to find a message that appears to question one of his postings. John feels his expertise—his entire Internet identity—is being challenged. The poster, Suzy Duran Duran Fan, didn't actually mean to question John's post at all, but without verbal cues and facial expressions, John reads it differently than she intended. He overreacts, and posts a message making some references to Suzy's questionable parentage. He finds it very easy to send because he is responding to words on a screen, not a human being.

You might think that "getting it all out" would make John feel better. It doesn't. Recent studies have shown that venting actually makes people angrier. Waiting through the time lapse for her response doesn't help. When John logs back in, still angry, he sees that Suzy now has a few thoughts of her own relating to John's parentage. The interesting thing is, the more out of line John's original post was, the more likely he is to be offended at the reply. The theory of cognitive dissonance says that we feel uncomfortable when we do something that is not in line with our own morals or beliefs about ourselves. John believes himself to be a reasonable and polite person.

Instead of acknowledging that he lost it, he will get to work to modify his perceptions of the other person so he can continue to feel he was in the right.

"Given how eager we are to justify our aggressive acts, and how skimpy the cues are about someone who offends us on the Internet," Wallace wrote, "it isn't difficult to guess that we would paint a very negative picture of the target we just reproached."

The ground is laid for an ever-escalating flame war.

INTERRUPTING OR
LET ME FINISH MY
SENTENCE OR YOU DIE

Don't you hate it when—excuse me I was talking—when people interrupt you while you're speaking?

"It's one thing if you interrupt to say 'the building's burning down,' but if it's not an emergency situation it's very rude," says Dr. Katherine Hawkins of the Elliott School of Communications at Wichita State University. "If I have the floor in a business meeting, and I'm trying

to express my point of view and you keep jumping in and negating everything I said, you might just as well have punched me. It's violating an expectation about rules of conversation."

We are all part of a speech community. As part of this community we know the unwritten rules of conversation. We give each other cues when it's time to speak or time to listen. When you're speaking and another person wants to jump in, she will incline her body forward, raise her eyebrows and take an audible breath. She's saying, "I'm taking a breath because I'm about to say something."

If you're not ready to give up the floor, you will avoid eye contact and fill up the gaps in your speech with "ums" and "uhs" to keep her from jumping in. If you are done speaking, you will signal her by letting your voice trail off and making eye contact. You may even make a gesture in her direction.

There is also something called "back channel communication." These are the grunts and noises of encouragement we make while another person is talking. We nod and insert "uh-huhs" at appropriate intervals.

"This is saying, 'I'm listening. This is interesting. Keep talking,' but if you speed up the back channel communication it's like saying 'Finish your turn. Finish your turn. I want to talk,'" Hawkins says.

You might be interested to know that a pushy conversational style not only gets on the nerves of other speakers, it affects the health of the dominating speaker as well. A 22-year study of 750 white, middle-class men carried out by Duke University Medical Center, ranked the subjects by their behavior characteristics including verbal competitiveness, loudness and self-aggrandizement. They monitored them taking other health risks into account. The researchers found that those who dominate conversations were 60 percent more likely to die at an earlier age than their more deferential peers. No word on how many were beaten to death by frustrated people who wanted to get a word in edgewise.

JUNK MAIL THROUGH **KEYBOARD CRUD**

JUNK MAIL

/K

The average American gets 22 pieces of mail each week. How many of these are personal? One. If you visit your local post office, you will proba-bly see a huge trash can where the people with P.O. Boxes can dump half of what comes in. There's a good chance you open your mail, if you open it, over the trash as well.

As of 1998, according to *USA Today*, U.S. households were receiving about 70,000,000,000 pieces of advertising mail a year. It steals our time and attention, but doesn't quite make our blood boil like telemarketers or e-mail spam.

"Direct mail lies somewhere in the middle of the nuisance scale," wrote Cheryl Russel in *American Demographics*. "Traditional etiquette says that it's rude to interrupt. Advertising that waits to be invited, rather than barging in, is more polite."

In fact, one of the reasons more people don't ask to have all our

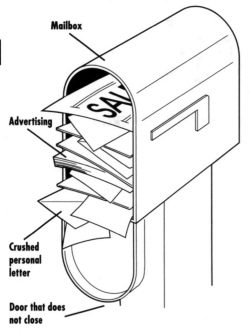

Mailbox

Advertising

Crushed personal letter

Door that does not close

third class mail blocked is that most of us like at least some of the junk we get. Under a law from the 1950s that is still in effect, anyone can go to the post office and fill out a form to attach to any piece of offensive junk mail. If that sender keeps you on its list, it is subject to criminal prosecution. You can also sign up for the Direct Marketing Associations Mail Preference Service, which will stem the tides of junk mail once DMA member companies update their records and learn you don't want to hear from them.

Yet 33 percent of those who signed up for the service said, in a 1992 survey, that they would prefer to get some advertising mail. If possible, they would like to pick and choose the categories of ads that come to their homes. The US Postal Service did its own study and found that Americans read more than 88 percent of the direct mail they get. Between 14 and 18 percent say they respond to offers they receive. What marketers have found is that we hate junk mail, but if we're interested in a particular catalog or advertisement, we don't mentally categorize it as "junk." As long as it keeps working, companies will keep sending us special offers.

KEYBOARD CRUD

See also sour milk

First the "s" key stopped working, then the letter "d." They're stuck in place by a plaster of cracker crumbs, skin oil and shed hairs. There may be strange new life forms evolving in there. The more time you spend at your computer, the more sticky and icky the keys can become. As more of us are trying to cram

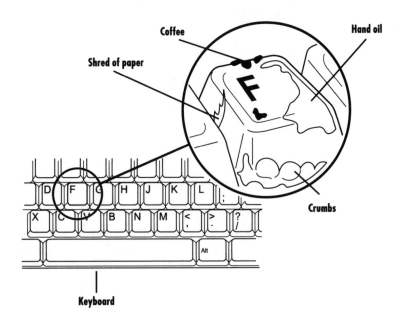

Coffee

Hand oil

Shred of paper

Crumbs

Keyboard

extra hours into our work day by eating lunch at our work station, keyboard crumbs become more and more common.

Keyboard crud makes your work space a little less pleasant, but is easily remedied. You don't need to buy fancy keyboard vacuums or air blowers (although you can if you like gadgets). Many keyboard problems can be avoided by covering the keyboard when it's not in use, especially if your computer is at a home that you share with children.

The crumbs that do find their way into the keyboard can be shaken out. Unplug the keyboard, hold it upside down and shake it firmly about once a week. You can clean the plastic with a soft cloth lightly moistened with cleaner. Spray the cleaner on the cloth, not directly on the keyboard.

Coffee on the keyboard? Unplug it right away, turn it upside down and wait for it to dry. That is, if you take your coffee black. Cream and sugar? It's probably time to get a new keyboard, unless you enjoy the smell of sour milk.

J/K

L

LASER POINTER THROUGH **LOST LUGGAGE**

LASER POINTERS

See also improvements that make things worse, powerpointization of the world

They've been called the "spitball of the 90s," those keychain laser pointers that kids use to project red dots onto teachers, movie screens, rock concert stages and each other. Paul Stanley of the band Kiss has stronger words for people who beam performers. "If any of those [explicative] want to come on the stage, I'll do them a service only a proctologist could do."

Laser pointers came on the market for corporate execs who wanted something a little more impressive than a stick to highlight their PowerPoint presentations. Originally, they cost between $80 and $100, which pretty much kept them out of the hands of the average teenager. But in the late 90s, point-

ers started to sell for as little as $9. That made them available to anyone who wanted to play backyard laser tag, "torture the cat" or the ever popular "who is pointing that damn laser at me?"

Beam from laser pointer from as far away as a 1/4 mile

The tiny beam of red light from a laser pointer can travel more than a quarter of a mile, making it hard to identify the beamer. "Kids like it because it's something you can annoy people with," gift shop owner Gus Rogers told the *Christian Science Monitor*. And annoyed people are. There is the theater owner in Elcamp, Texas, who had to stop a showing of *Bride of Chucky* because there were too many red dots on the screen and the New Jersey Transit driver who swerved off the road when someone shined a laser into his rearview mirror. The bus, loaded with 27 passengers, nearly crashed into a telephone pole.

According to the *Christian Science Monitor*, "dotting" police officers has become a popular hobby in some areas. Police say they can't tell the prankster from a dangerous criminal with a laser site on his rifle. Ophthalmologists warn that lasers can damage vision when fired into people's eyes, as some young people have done in highly publicized cases.

Fans of laser pointers say the health dangers have been blown out of proportion and that the 5 milliwatt capacity of most pointers presents a very small risk. They argue that most of the cases where eye damage occurred involved some rather reckless behavior—shining the laser directly into the eye for a long period of time to see if the pupil would contract, for example.

Even so, many municipalities have passed laws banning the sale of pointers to minors or in some cases to anyone. In 1997 the British government, citing health risks, ordered stores to stop selling lasers with beams more powerful than one milliwatt to anyone but a qualified operator.

Those who sell the light pens argue the red dot fad will run out of steam of its own accord and legislation is not necessary. If they're right, expect to see laser pens at every garage sale, a victim of changing tastes, like Rubik's cubes circa 1990.

LEGROOM ON AIRPLANES, OR THE SEATBACK IN YOUR FACE

See also airline delays, airline food, armrest wars, ears popping, foot's asleep, lost luggage, standing too close

You're in the middle seat. Your bag is stowed under the seat in front of you, which means you can't stretch your feet out in front of you—unless you call putting your tootsies a couple of inches forward "stretching." Your neighbors have taken both armrests and now the guy in the seat in front of you decides to lean his seat all the way back. Your thimble-sized cup of coffee is now on your lap, and you have about as much freedom of movement as a body in a coffin.

In November 2000, the media began to focus great attention on what they dubbed "economy class syndrome." The spark was a well-publicized story about a British woman in her late 20s who dropped dead after a 20 hour flight from Australia to London's Heathrow Airport. Doctors attributed her death to deep venous thrombosis—a blood clot had developed in her leg and traveled to one of her lungs.

Many medical experts dispute the link between cramped seats

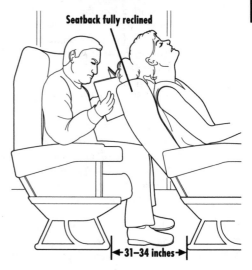

ECONOMY CLASS

Seatback fully reclined

31–34 inches

L

and deep venous thrombosis. The medical journal *Lancet* published a report by Dutch and Italian researchers that found no such correlation.

Still, the papers had a field day with "economy class syndrome." The public wants it to exist because we want to have a documented, medical reason to convince airlines to give us a place to put our legs. Travel, for those of us back in the steerage class, is uncomfortable and psychologically stressful because other people are planted well within our bounds of personal space.

"Quite frankly, I don't think this issue would even exist if we passed a law that required all executives of the nation's airlines to fly in the middle seat on coach," said Alaska Senator Frank Murkowski.

The FAA does have regulations as to the configuration of the seats. They must be designed to insure that all passengers can exit an aircraft in an emergency within a specified period of time. There are no regulations that assure minimum comfort.

Until the 1980s, the distance between your seat back and the one in front of you was 34 inches. Many carriers have cut that down to 31 or 32. The airlines say the seat back cushions just aren't as deep, you haven't lost legroom. It just seems more crowded because the airplanes are fuller.

But here's the thing, as much as we love to complain about the lack of legroom, unpalatable airline food and having to pay for movie headsets (come on, I paid $400 for this ticket and you can't give me a headset for free?), we want our travel to be cheap. We buy airline tickets by calling a travel agent or going on line and seeking out the lowest price. If we searched for the airline with the most legroom, the airlines would have to offer more space to be competitive. As it is, to get our economy class business, they have to offer the cheapest ticket. The airlines aren't raking in huge profits compared to other industries. In 1998, a very good year for the airlines, the industry turned only a $5 billion profit on $100 billion in revenues—just 5 percent. As long as passengers count their nickels and dimes when buying tickets, the airlines will find ways to cut nickels and dimes from their cost. That means they're likely to keep cramming in as many seats as they can.

LINES: THE OTHER ONE IS ALWAYS FASTER

See also caught in traffic, road rage

You just want to get up to the cash register, but all these people are in your way. They don't deserve to get up to the register as much as you do. Waiting is aggravating, and worse still is seeing someone who got in line later pass you by.

We spend a lot of time waiting around in line. The research firm Priority Management estimates we spend five years of our lives waiting. That's five years you'll never get back, and you certainly don't want to see someone else passing you up and getting that two minutes of life advantage.

MIT professor Richard C. Larson teaches a seminar on "queuing theory" and the "psychology of lines." He believes stores should always have one long line in-

stead of several short ones. With short lines you have what he calls "slips and skips." The slips happen when somebody

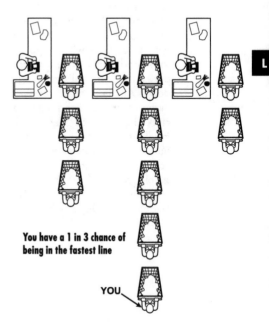

You have a 1 in 3 chance of being in the fastest line

YOU

moves ahead of you. Skips are when you move ahead of them. We're thrilled when we get to skip ahead, but the pleasure is outweighed by the disgust at slipping.

"When somebody slips by you, your psychological cost is high," he told the *Washington Post.* "You're going to remember that."

If you think this is just a case of negative thinking—think again. Chances are the line next to you really will finish first. Let's say you're at the grocery and there are five lines open. It's true that on average the lines will move at more or less the same rate over time. One will be going faster and then the coupon clipper of the year will bog things down. Another will be cruising along at record speed until the clerk shouts "price check!" All in all they tend to average out, but that probably won't help you much. It comes down to simple odds. Of the five lines, only one can be the speediest. Therefore, you have only a one

in five chance of getting into it. Even if you just consider the lanes to either side of you, you have only a one in three chance of being in the fastest. More often than not, then, the other guy will be asked "paper or plastic" before you.

One other fact to keep in mind when waiting in line—let's say you're at the department of motor vehicles to renew your drivers license along with half of the people in the state. As you wait in line, you get more and more impatient and aggravated. When you get to the front of the line you snap, "I've been waiting in line for an hour!" The clerk snaps back at you, "No you haven't this line is only 15 minutes long!" Guess what? You're both wrong. According to the 1989 study "Misperceptions of Time in Sales Transactions," published in *Advances in Consumer Research,* 77 percent of customers overestimate the amount of time they spend waiting, and 84 percent of employees underestimate it.

LOST LUGGAGE

See also airline food, airline delays, armrest wars, legroom on airplanes

A flight to Paris. That's what your luggage got. Unfortunately, your flight was to Idaho. You stood there watching the bags circle on the baggage claim conveyor until the selection was down to one purple suitcase—not yours.

To be fair to the airlines, most bags end up where they're supposed to. Only half a percent to one percent of bags are mishandled or misrouted according to the Department of Transportation. When you consider the number of passengers who fly each day, though, one percent adds up. About 10,000 to 20,000 bags are mishandled each day. Department of Transportation records show that United Airlines has the worst

track record when it comes to mishandled bags.

"It's not that the bag is lost," a United Airlines spokesman once said, "It fails to make a flight."

There are many factors that can cause your bag to have a different final destination than you do. Often bags don't show up because the traveler arrived late and just made it on the plane. The suitcase wasn't as fast. Weather can tie up traffic at major hubs and cause confusion for baggage handlers. Sometimes bags get damaged. A handle can come off taking its destination tag with it, or a tag can come off leaving a bag unidentified. Occasionally the culprit is human error. Someone can type in a wrong letter at check-in producing a code for a distant airport. Then there was the case of the Texas couple who routinely walked into the

Dallas Fort Worth airport and took random bags off the claim carousels so they could sell the contents at a flea market.

With computer tracking, in most cases, travelers are reunited with their luggage within 24 hours. Often the airline knows the bag was misrouted before you do. Gate agents, baggage agents and customer service representatives can check a piece of luggage with a hand-held terminal to make sure it is on route. If it's not where it's supposed to be, they can call ahead to your destination airport and have you paged. You won't have your stuff, but you'll know where it is.

If the bag has been more seriously misplaced, the airlines search for it with an international tracer system to which 275 airlines subscribe. If the bag doesn't show up in the system within five days, the luggage is declared untraceable, but it usually isn't considered irretrievably lost for 30 days. At that point (or if a mangled bag turns up in the meantime), the airline will settle with you. In December 2000, the airlines increased the cap for lost or damaged luggage to $2,500 from $1,250. There is no law requiring compensation for temporarily lost bags.

When all else fails, bags without identification are opened and airline personnel search for something inside—personal documents, prescriptions, library books—to let them know whom the suitcase belongs to. When that fails, the bags are kept for a period of time. Air Canada's Central Baggage Tracing Office, for example, keeps lost bags for six months. Then where do they go? They're sold. In America, they end up in Scottsboro, Alabama. In Canada, the bounty can be found at The Unclaimed Luggage and Goods Store in Ottawa. The prices airlines charge these dealers vary; some charge per bag, others by the pound. The U.S. store features 7,000 new items a day. It's online store front, www.unclaimedbaggage.com, is updated with 200 items a day.

If you would prefer to keep your clothes and accessories out of the hands of the bargain hunters here are a few tips—invest in a bag that has a slide-in window for ID cards. If the handle comes off, your contact information will still be there. Be sure the contact information on your bags is up to date and include a card with your address and phone number inside the suitcase.

MAPS THROUGH **MOVIE TRAILERS**

MAPS: YOUR DESTINATION IS ALWAYS IN THE FOLD

See also road rage

Y ou're in Vermont. Problem is, you're supposed to be in Connecticut. You're stopped at the side of the road with a map unfolded on the hood of your car. Your destination city, of course, falls right in the middle of a fold, which bends some

M

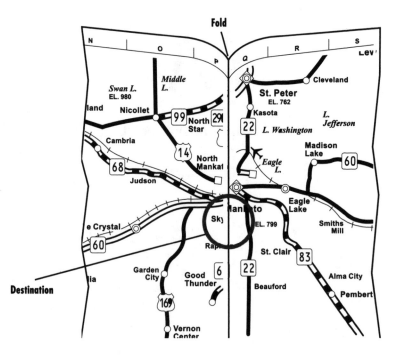

of the main roads in odd directions. Two Cows, Vermont, where you now stand, is right along the edge of the map, partially obscured by the legend.

Why is it that the place you need to find always seems to be in an awkward part of the map? Geometry, says Robert Matthews, a scientist who has devoted himself to proving the validity of Murphy's Law. In his article "Murphy's Law of Maps" which appeared in *Teaching Statistics*, Matthews defined a "Murphy Zone" around the edge of the map and along the edges of the central crease. Because the zone corresponds to the outermost dimension of the map, it is also the largest. A relatively narrow width makes up a comparatively large total area. While the Murphy Zone takes up about one tenth the width of the total page, the odds of a random point falling

in that area is better than 50:50.

If you're not able to follow the math, you can experiment yourself. Pick 100 random locations from a map's index and see how many land in the Murphy area. More often than not it will fall in an awkward place. With a few more calculations, Matthews was able to determine that one in four of all trips will both begin and end in a Murphy Zone. If your path does not begin or end there, chances are, some vital juncture will be hidden in the fold. In other words, if your trip route can correspond with the worst possible part of the map, it will. If you'd like to look over Matthew's equations yourself, his original article appears on his Web page at http://ourworld.compuserve.com/homepages/rajm/mapfull.htm.

M

MEDICAL GIBBERISH OR YOU HAVE PERMISSION TO REMOVE MY WHAT?

See also hernia exams

When your doctor spells something out for you in writing, do you understand it? Probably not. The medical journal *Surgery* recently reviewed more than 600 medical consent forms from hospitals around the country. These are the forms that give your surgeon permission to cut into various parts of your anatomy. The researchers concluded that the documents failed to provide such information as alternatives to surgery.

Of greater concern is the fact that much of the information is unintelligible to the average patient. The doctors who write the text probably have much more education than you do. The researchers found that in order to understand about a quarter of the documents, a patient must have at least a college education.

Beyond that, try to read your doctor's prescription. You might have trouble just making out the writing. A report published in the *British Medical Journal* reveals it's no myth: Doctors, as a group, have illegible handwriting. A team of researchers had 92 doctors, nurses and administrators carefully write their names, the alphabet and the numbers zero to nine. They ran the results through an optical scanner that picked out unrecognizable letters. The results:

The nurses had the best writing of the bunch, followed by the administrators. Doctors had almost twice the error rate of the other groups. The *Journal* concluded, "Doctors, even when asked to be as neat as possible, produce handwriting that is worse than that of other professions." As if that weren't bad enough, when researchers examined pens from

42 doctors in 1999, they found 15 different kinds of bacteria on them. If the pen itself doesn't kill you, watch out for a misread prescription!

In 1996, *Journal of the American Medical Association* reported that the annual number of deaths from hospital errors in the U.S. is four times the number of deaths from automobile crashes and exceeds that from all other accidents combined.

Clearly printed name of doctor

Description of drug with dosage and explanation of how many to take a day

M

MIMES

A recent issue of *Entertainment Weekly* asked celebrities about the worst jobs they ever had. Robin Williams needed no time to come up with his answer. He once worked as a mime in New York City.

"Kids would try to kick you," he said. "But the scariest people were the rich older ladies... they would very dryly say, 'Get the [explicative] away from me.' I would get Vuitton bags in the face."

A complex mix of social and psychological factors come into play when we're confronted with a guy in white face paint walking against the wind inside an invisible box. We're affected by xenophobia (it's a French thing), class consciousness, a feeling of a loss of power and our childhood fear of clowns. All of this translates into anger and even violent fantasies. (How often are professional mimes asked, "If I shoot you, should I use a silencer?")

Fear of clowns is common enough to warrant its own name—coulrophobia. Psychologists say people love and hate clowns and mimes for the same reason—the mask that hides the real features and allows a person to behave unpredictably. Will he jump into the audience and make fun of you? He might. When he is performing, he is in control. That means you are not.

Some people hate clowns because of traumatic childhood experiences. They remember being confronted with a big, painted person with purple hair and humongous feet and running in terror. "Kids can't quite process it," Jerilyn Ross, director of the Ross Center for Anxiety and Related Disorders, told the Washington Post. "They know it's a person, but it doesn't look like one. It's disorienting for them."

People who are bothered by clowns, however, are not as vocal as mime haters. This has to do with the history of modern mime. The French combined mime with ballet and elevated it to the status of high art. Americans are naturally suspicious of anything that reeks of high culture, especially if they fail to understand it. We also have stereotypes about the French, whom we suspect are looking down their noses at us. While the average American can easily avoid opera, ballet and art galleries, mimes often perform in parks and public places.

We're not looking for art at that moment. So what we see is a person in disguise as a very pale Frenchman, who could speak but probably believes himself to be above it, who might start making fun of us at any moment... Where's that silencer when you need it?

Exaggerated facial expression of surprise

M

MOSQUITOES

See also ants, cockroaches, fleas, flies, gnats

There are few things about the mosquito that are not annoying to humans. There is the buzzing, the itching welts they leave behind and their habit of spoiling picnics and barbeques. The fact that they drink blood and in the process transmit disease goes beyond annoying to dangerous.

Mosquitoes, as it turns out, are the most formidable transmitters of disease in the animal kingdom. In various parts of the world they spread malaria, encephalitis, yellow fever, dengue, elephantitis, the West Nile virus and dog heartworm. Fortunately, they cannot transmit AIDS. A mosquito that bites an HIV positive individual does not hold enough of the virus to infect another person. In America, only one mosquito in 1,000 car-ries disease organisms, which is a great relief unless you happen to be bitten by the one.

In fairness, it is only a part of the population that gives the rest of the mosquito community a bad rap. Mosquito men never bite. It is only the female who sucks blood when she needs the nutrients to develop fertile eggs. The rest of the time, both male and female mosquitoes are satisfied with sugar from plant nectar. Each time a female does snack on an animal's blood, she puts herself at risk of being swatted and killed, so she avoids the blood feast until absolutely necessary.

Humans are not even her favorite choice of host. She prefers the taste of birds, rodents and large mammals like cows and horses. If those delicacies are unavailable, however, she is happy to snack on a person.

She knows where you are because you breathe. Mosquitoes can detect carbon dioxide from up to 40 miles away, according to some sources. She localizes a breathing animal by flying in a zigzag fashion across the stream of CO_2. As she approaches, she sniffs for water vapor and lactic acid which tell her that the source is an animal and not, say, a smokestack. When she gets close enough, she uses her other senses. She observes movement and detects the infra-red radiation emitted by warm bodies.

She has no illusions that you will welcome her visit, so she tries her best to land in a place that is hard to swat—and consequently hard to scratch. Sometimes, though, she gives herself away with the tell-tale whine of her wings which beat up to 500 cycles a second. If she does manage to avoid detection, she searches the skin's surface with her stylet until she finds a capillary. Then she punctures the skin with four of her six probes. The other two are then used like a straw to slurp up the blood meal.

Her saliva keeps the blood from clotting and also serves as an anesthetic, which is important to the mosquito because it takes up to five minutes to complete her meal. The anesthetic helps

M

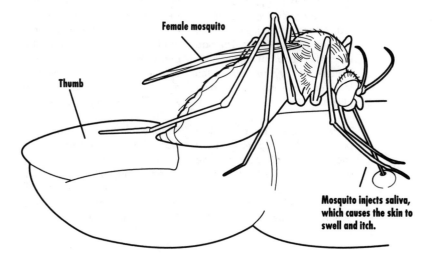

Female mosquito

Thumb

Mosquito injects saliva, which causes the skin to swell and itch.

her avoid detection. The swollen, itchy welts that appear after she leaves are caused by an allergic reaction to the saliva. It takes about three minutes from the time she bites you for the spot to start itching.

There is a popular myth that if you let the mosquito drink her fill she will remove the anticoagulant before she leaves and the bite will not itch. There is no truth to this, but there is at least one reason to let a mosquito finish. If she has not drank her fill she may come back. The result is two welts, not one.

If you seem to be a person who is particularly attractive to the pests, there is good news and bad news. The good news is you're not crazy, mosquitoes really do favor the taste of some individuals over others. The bad news is, you're not crazy, mosquitoes really do favor the taste of some individuals over others.

Why do they prefer certain people? Well, scientists don't know everything. So far, they are only able to prove that they do.

The best way to keep mosquitoes at bay is to rid the environment of their breeding ground—standing water. The mosquito's hunting ground is about 100–200 feet from where she begins her life cycle. If she breeds far away, she'll bite far away too.

Some swear that high doses of the B vitamin thiamine or garlic pills can make a person unattractive to the pests. For those who prefer to avoid commercial repellants with DEET, there are a number of natural deterrents you can try. Pennyroyal essential oil, peppermint, vanilla, bay, clove, sassafras and cedar all have their adherents. You could try burning rosemary and sage on your next barbeque—some swear this keeps mosquitoes at bay. Some rub fresh parsley or apple cider vinegar on the skin. Another homemade bug repellant can be concocted with 1 tablespoon citronella oil, 2 cups white vinegar, 1 cup water and 1 cup Avon Skin-So-Soft bath oil.

If none of these preparations works for you, your best bet is to figure out who among your friends is most attractive to mosquitoes and invite him to all your outdoor parties. Be sure he stands near you.

MOTION SICKNESS

See also stupid warning labels

Ah sailing. The fresh sea air. The lapping of the sea against the hull. The rocking back and forth and back and forth and... Oh no! Why is it that you can ride your bike without getting sick, but on the boat, or in the back seat of a car your stomach contents come up?

When you walk down the street you never get walk-sick. But when you're in a big vehicle, especially if you're not driving, things change. Inside an aircraft, for example, the fluid in your ears shifts as the plane rises and sinks. This signals your brain that your body is in motion. Your eyes, however, are telling a different story. They aren't perceiving a lot of movement. They tell your brain that you're in a big room sitting in an uncomfortable chair reading a magazine. This confuses the brain. The brain hates to be confused, so it sends out stress hormones like adrenaline. The stomach is especially susceptible to stress cues and it contracts. With luck you make it to the airsick bag on time.

3-by-5-inch opening of air sickness bag

M

The best way to avoid motion discomfort is to look out the window or go up on deck so your eyes will be on the same wavelength as your ears. Avoid reading in a vehicle and don't travel on an empty stomach. It increases queasiness. If you fly, choose a seat over the wing on the right side of the plane. Most flight patterns turn left, so you won't be jostled around as much if you sit on the right.

Then again, if it weren't for motion discomfort, Charles Sant of Bracknell England wouldn't have a hobby. Sant collects airline sick bags. How does an otherwise serious service information analyst find himself collecting such a unique item? Believe it or not, he was drawn into the hobby 10 years ago by a fellow collector.

Since then, he has amassed enough bags to make his former classmate absolutely ill. His collection has doubled to more than 200 since he launched his unique web page "Mementos to Motion Discomfort" (http:/ to Motion Discomfort" (http:/

/www.sant.demon.co.uk/ sickbag.html). The web presence allows him to swap selected sick sacks with fellow enthusiasts, and yes, there are many. The Yahoo search engine has an entire category devoted to airsick bag collectors.

Some of the most interesting variations in Sant's collection include those from defunct airlines, bags made out of blotting paper, bags with games on the back, a bag that doubles as an envelope for a film development company, an almost transparent bag, an airline with separate business and economy-class airsick bags and even a sack that carries the curious caution: "When used, this bag may contain biohazardous waste."

So far there are no price guides for sack collectors, and no conventions have yet been planned, but the time may come up. If you are inspired to start a collection and would like to trade, Sant has 23 surplus British Airways airsick bags he'd love to exchange with you.

MOVIE TRAILERS THAT GIVE THE WHOLE PLOT AWAY

About three-fourths of the way into the blockbuster film *Titanic*, the female lead Rose (Kate Winslet) says good-bye to her new found love Jack Dawson (Leonardo DiCaprio). She looks at him with longing as her life raft is lowered. Will they be parted forever? No, of course not! You know they won't because you saw the pre-view and Rose and Jack cling to the rail of the ship together as it sinks into the sea. So much for suspense.

"Today, if I had to cut the trailer for *Citizen Kane*, they would probably make me ex-plain what Rosebud is," said one editor. "But by that point they'd probably have changed Rosebud to Jen because the name Rosebud didn't test well among women 18 to 34."

These days studios don't wait around long to see if a movie is a hit or a bomb. If it doesn't do big box office numbers the first weekend, it's headed straight to video. So the studios start promoting the films earlier and earlier with thrill ride trailers. They're called "trailers", by the way, because in the old days

M

Trailer, before featured presentation

they used to play them after the feature film. Now they're up front where there is more of a captive audience. The purpose of the trailer is to get large numbers of people into the theater in that all important first weekend. If you went, but complained about the trailer later, you still bought a ticket and the studio is happy.

Some critics say the tell-all previews are part of a Hollywood trend away from subtlety. The studios, the argument goes, believe you won't go to a movie unless everything is spelled out for you. Call it a McDonald's mentality. If you don't know in advance exactly what to expect, you turn to entertainment you know and feel comfortable with—which may be the competition's entertainment.

Others blame *Sesame Street* and MTV which raised a generation that expects fast edits. In the past, a trailer had maybe 75 scenes. Now it has roughly 125, which means much more of the story is revealed. A preview must be eye catching, quick and stunning or it might not be seen at all. They cost an average of $300,000 to make and for every trailer that a theater owner decides to run, there

are another seven or eight that you never see.

Even if a preview doesn't tell the whole story, it can often be misleading. Sometimes you go into the theater expecting an action thriller only to find yourself viewing a romance. That is because the trailer makers create different versions of the preview to air during different television programs. The version that airs during Oprah will play up the romance. The one that airs during *Monday Night Football* will piece together all the action sequences. Of course, if you watch a variety of programming, the combined effect will give even more of the plot away.

One of the worst preview teases is the trailer that looks as though it's a laugh-a-minute or a thrill-a-minute film. After you shell out your $8-$10, on a ticket you find that the great moments in the two-minute preview were the only watchable two minutes of the film.

"It's hard to find a two-hour movie that doesn't have two minutes of good trailer material," editor Phil Daccord once said. "But do I ever feel guilty? Yes, I do."

NOISE THROUGH **NYLONS**

NOISE

See also booming car stereos, car alarms, finger nails on the blackboard

Your neighbor loves to blast heavy metal music on his stereo. How can he stand to listen to that noise? You'd rather listen to a washing machine that is out of balance. Scientists have attempted to quantify the annoyance factor of sounds with a noise scale, NOY. The problem is that there is little agreement among research subjects as to what is sound and what is noise. Noises are usually loud, for example, but loudness alone does not make a sound annoying to all listeners—just ask the audience at a rock concert.

What experts generally agree upon is that noise is bad for you. Various studies of traffic and aircraft sounds near major airports have concluded that hearing loss, sleep disorders, elevated blood pressure, heart disease and psychological trauma can be brought on by exposure to noise. In 1979, researchers at the London Institute of Psychiatry reviewed the findings of two studies conducted near London's Heathrow Airport. The studies had compared rates of admission at Springfield Psychiatric Hospital and found that areas closest to the airport, with higher levels of noise, also had the highest rates of hospital admission. Other studies have correlated high noise areas with poor reading and math scores in school-age children.

The 1957 study, *Noise in Relation to Annoyance, Performance and Mental Health* by D. Broadbent, concluded that sudden, unexpected noise causes the heart to race, blood pressure to rise and the muscles to contract.

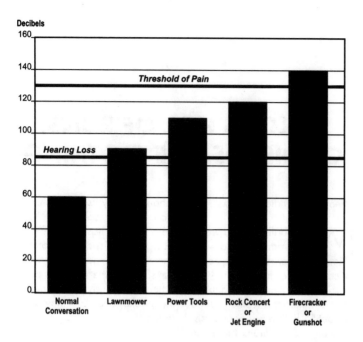

Decibels

160
140 — Threshold of Pain
120
100
80 — Hearing Loss
60
40
20
0

Normal Conversation | Lawnmower | Power Tools | Rock Concert or Jet Engine | Firecracker or Gunshot

Following a loud bang, digestion, stomach contractions, and the flow of gastric juices all stop.

Appropriately enough, the word "noise" is a distant cousin of the word "nausea." Both evolved out of the Greek *nautia* and Latin *navis*, or ship. Nausea was originally used specifically to describe seasickness. Eventually, it was applied to similar discomfort on land. The related word, "noise," in Latin once was used to describe the fuss surrounding a sick person. In old French it was transformed into an expression for loud disagreement. This term came into English where it was applied to any unpleasant sound.

Researchers at Northwestern University who studied the sounds that make people cringe found that fingernails on a blackboard was, by far, the most universally annoying. What was the second most aggravating noise, according to their subjects? It was the sound of two pieces of Styrofoam rubbing together.

N

NYLONS FULL OF RUNS, OR DISPOSABLE CLOTHING

See also unmatched socks

Whose brilliant idea was it that women should wear flimsy, run-prone pantyhose? According to the National Association of Hosiery Manufacturers, American women spend about $2 billion a year on sheer hosiery—$2 billion. Note the language they use: "The American woman consumed 11.6 pairs of sheer hosiery in 1992." Consumed. Disposable clothes. The average pair lasts three days. That's the average pair. Often they barely make it out of the package before they start to run.

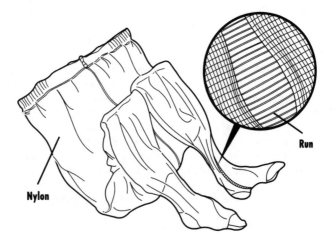

Run

Nylon

Ironically, the name Nylon was actually derived from the expression "No Run." When DuPont created the first man-made fiber, a committee was put to work on naming it. They were going to go with No Run, until someone pointed out that they did, in fact, run. (Another rejected name was Duparooh, short for DuPont Pulls A Rabbit Out of a Hat.) They didn't run quite as much as silk stockings, which accounts for their popularity, even though they were initially twice as expensive. Patriotism also helped sell Nylon: Silk came from Japan, and the U.S. was soon to enter World War II.

"So long as skirts are up and women are vain, silk stockings will remain an important part of the feminine wardrobe," silk stocking makers boasted. By 1948, 85 percent of all hosiery was nylon.

As long as women insist on wearing a skin-like flimsy garment, they're going to have to deal with runs, says Frank Oswald, marketing consultant for Du Pont, one of the world's largest suppliers of hosiery yarns. "Women have to realize this is the thinnest garment on their bodies, and it's covering half their body," he told *Newsday*. Opaque tights and thicker fibers like Lycra and spandex do not run as much, but they feel heavier.

What can you do to keep stockings from running? Not a lot. Once a snag hits, you can stop it temporarily with clear nail polish or hair spray. Another helpful hint is to cut the leg off of a pair and wait for another pair to get a run in the opposite leg. The law of averages says eventually you should have two runless legs. You can then slip on both half-pairs as one. Although some women swear keeping nylons in the freezer makes them run resistant, it's not true. It just makes them cold.

N

OFFICE CUBICLES THROUGH **OVERPLAYED MUSIC**

OFFICE CUBICLES, OR FATTENED UP IN THE CUBE FARM

See also noise, telemarketers

Once people had real offices. Walls. Remember walls? If you're under the age of 45 you probably don't. Since 1968, employees have been surrounded by dividers. They keep you from seeing, but not hearing, the person next to you. If your office is busy, the important client you are calling just might hang up because she hears the cacophony of voices

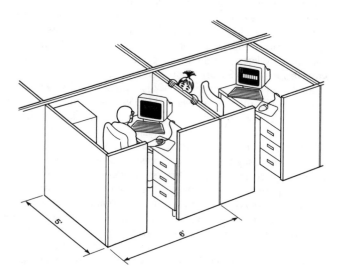

in the background and thinks you're a telemarketer.

Not only do you not have walls or a door, you probably have less space than you used to. Until recently a standard office enclosure measured 8 feet by 8 feet. These days suppliers report that they're selling cubes as small as 5 feet by 6 feet, affording employees 30 square feet of workspace. That's about twice as much space as a funeral casket and half as much as a jail cell.

Having an office door is a sign of status today. The *Washington Post* reported that this is true even when the practice is illogical. "For example, social workers or admitting nurses in hospitals may really need private offices to interview clients," wrote reporter Curt Suplee. "But often the only private offices belong to the supervisor, who never conducts interviews."

When you can't close a door, you can't as easily control your personal space. Imposing desks keep people at a more formal distance. As with other issues of personal space, office arrangements vary by culture. In England they place less importance on the size of the office because status is more clearly evident in a person's accent. In Germany and Switzerland, workers tend to keep their office doors closed, whereas in America, most people keep their office doors open unless there is a particular need for privacy—a "closed door meeting."

That doesn't mean we can waltz in and out of an office at will. We behave as though there were an invisible barrier where the closed door would be. We knock on the door frame or clear our throats or lean inside just a bit with our feet well outside the entrance.

If you don't rank office door status, chances are you're being bombarded with noises that increase your stress. A 2001 study by environmental psychologist Gary Evans of Cornell University compared 40 secretaries. Half worked in a quiet setting, half in a noisy office. Those subjected to constant office noise had higher levels of stress (as measured by the presence of the stress hormone epinephrine in the urine) and made 40 percent fewer attempts to solve an unsolvable puzzle. They also made fewer adjustments to their seating, which put them at higher risk for repetitive stress injuries.

OVERPLAYED MUSIC, OR IF I HEAR THAT RICKY MARTIN SONG ONE MORE TIME...

You turn on the radio, it's that Ricky Martin song. It wasn't bad the first 50 times, but you're sick of it now. So you change the channel and hear that Ricky Martin song. You give up and flip on MTV and you hear that Ricky Martin song again. You get in your car and drive to the mall and Best Buy is playing that Ricky Martin song on its PA system. You wish Ricky Martin had never been born.

It's the same with the oldies. Thousands of great songs have been recorded in the past, but the same tired oldies surface again and again. On an average day, according to Tom Heymann's book of that title, the Rolling Stones' "Satisfaction" is played on the radio 302 times, Elvis's "Love Me Tender" is played 433 times and The Beatles' "Yesterday" is played 589 times—about 24 hours worth of "Yesterday."

What happened to variety? Why do all the radio stations sound the same? The answer is marketing. Radio stations do not earn their money by playing songs. They earn it by selling commercials. From a business point of view, a piece of music is just a tool to flush out a certain market niche. If you play music that captures the ear of the 18-35 demographic, you can sell advertising aimed to that group. If you want males of that age you might play album-oriented rock. If you want females, you might try Top 40. Want to sell to middle-aged women? Adult Contemporary and Country are good bets. In other words, the target demographic comes first, the music selection comes second.

Radio is a risky business. Most stations, especially the small ones, find it hard to turn a profit. So they do not leave their music

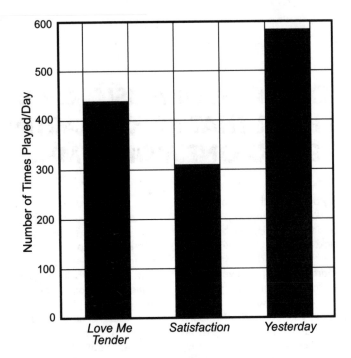

selection to chance. In large markets, radio stations pay for audience research to test the appeal of songs in their market. Some songs are selected based on the program director's judgment (so-called "earpicks"), but they are becoming increasingly rare. The more cautious choice is to rely on studies.

Smaller markets can't afford their own research, so they rely on the playlists of larger stations to guide them in programming decisions—that is, if they still

do their programming in house. Increasingly, local stations rely on programming provided by outside companies. Often, the music schedule is sent on a disc or series of discs that can be loaded right into a station's automation system. Other stations pick up programming provided by satellite.

In 1996, the Telecommunications Act increased the number of radio stations a single firm can own. Between March 1996 and February 1998 the number of owners dropped 14 percent as the number of stations grew by 3 percent. It is efficient and economical for the new radio goliaths to replace local newscasts with national and regional services and to use the same music programming in stations in various markets. The big-business approach is more musically cautious.

According to *USA Today,* the typical adult contemporary station 15 years ago would have 18 to 24 current hits on its playlist. Today, it probably plays 9–12 current hits. Some Top 40 stations play the same hits up to eight times a day. They don't do this to annoy us. As much as we complain about the repetition and the lack of variety, studies continue to show that we actually like to hear familiar music. When we hear an unfamiliar song, we might turn the dial in search of a familiar one. The one thing radio programmers don't want you to do is change channels. You might not switch back.

Radio consultant Lee Abrams defended the practice of market research in the *Dallas Morning News.* "We were actually going out into the streets and finding out what people wanted," he said. "I think the presumptuousness is in the underground DJs playing what they and their friends like."

Another reason music seems more homogenous has to do with how we shop. Big chains like Best Buy and Wal-Mart are competing with mom and pop record stores. The big chain stores offer CDs at bargain prices, sometimes even selling popular titles below wholesale to attract customers who will buy more expensive merchandise. The chains have limited shelf space and only stock hits. A typical Wal-Mart carries about 4,000 titles—a tiny fraction of the quarter million CD and cassettes that are commercially available. Their buyers, too, rely on market research, chart data and radio playlists.

Many media watchers believe the Internet will soon change all of this. The smallest station can now be heard world-wide. Artists create their own home pages where listeners can sample new songs that are shunned by radio programmers. Still, the technology has a way to go before it is a real threat to the current hierarchy. In the meantime, you'll just have to learn to love NSYNC.

PAPER CUTS THROUGH **POWERPOINTIZATION**

PAPER CUTS

You're handing a memo to the boss who wants everything in writing when, sliiiicccceeee... It slips past your finger cutting a gouge as it goes. Why is it that when you cut yourself shaving this morning you didn't feel a thing, but a flimsy piece of paper has you wincing and sucking your finger like a baby?

A razor cuts your skin smoothly and superficially. Paper cuts actually tear through your skin. The cuts are tiny but deceptively deep. As Dr. Ted Broadway of

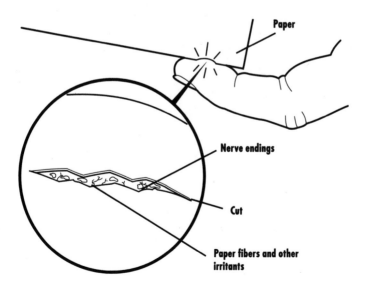

Paper

Nerve endings

Cut

Paper fibers and other irritants

P

the Ontario Medica Association explained to the *Toronto Star,* the cuts "just get into the layer of the nerve endings and irritates them. The friction of the tissue causes the nerve endings to go nuts. Every nerve is firing." The paper also contains more irritants than the razor. It leaves fibers and chemicals in the tiny wound.

Some people use superglue to seal paper cuts shut. Doctors have been using a medical grade superglue to repair skin lacerations for some time. The stuff you find at the hardware store was not specifically designed for the purpose, so you probably should not slather it over large, deep cuts, but dermatologists say it is not likely to be toxic on something as small as a paper cut. If you do try this method, be sure you let the glue dry before you pick anything else up. You definitely don't want to end up with a throbbing, sliced finger glued to a coffee cup.

P

PARKING LOT BATTLES, OR GET OUT OF MY SPACE!

See also armrest wars, caught in traffic, road rage

If cities are "urban jungles," parking lots are our territorial battle grounds. As soon as we see an open spot, we claim it in the name of our Ford Explorer.

We're willing to fight anyone who tries to prevent us from possessing it. A survey by Bernice Kanner, author of *Are You Normal*, asked Americans what they would do if they arrived at a parking spot at the same time as another driver. Almost two-

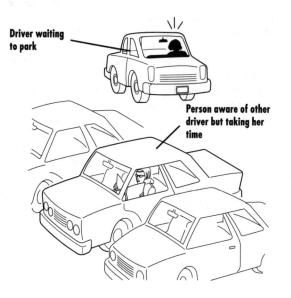

Driver waiting to park

Person aware of other driver but taking her time

P

thirds said they would fight for it. Northeastern drivers were the most stubborn; 79 percent said they'd rather fight than give up the space, compared to 40 percent of Midwesterners.

If your car is already comfortably entrenched in a space, the situation doesn't change much. Pennsylvania State University researchers Barry Ruback and Daniel Juieng conducted a study of more than 400 drivers at an Atlanta-area mall parking lot. They reported their findings in the article "Territorial Defense in Parking Lots: Retaliation Against Waiting Drivers" in the *Journal of Applied Social Psychology.*

They discovered departing drivers took seven seconds longer to get out of a spot when someone was waiting for it than when no one was there. If the waiting driver honked, the departing driver became even pokier. The wait jumped from 32.2 seconds (with no one waiting) to 43 seconds.

Men, unlike women, appeared to be affected by the type of car as well. If a $57,000 Infiniti Q45 pulled up, men got out of the way in 30 seconds; for a $5,200 station wagon, the wait was longer than 39 seconds.

No one seems immune to the parking lot war. Not even researcher Diane Nahl who has made a career out of teaching others to tame their aggressive driving impulses.

"I saw a woman in a parking lot the other day and she was parked across three spaces and reading a newspaper," Nahl said. "She wasn't concerned at all. The thoughts started coming, 'How dare she? Why is she so disrespectful?' Then I went up to the second floor, I looked down to the parking lot and saw that there was now a tow truck on the scene. I was completely unjust in my judgment but it's so automatic to be offended by what people do."

Like when you're coming up to what appears to be an empty space in a full parking lot only to discover there's a Volkswagen Bug wedged way up in the front so you can't see it until you're about to pull in....

POTHOLES, OR FASTEN YOUR SEATBELTS, WE'RE IN FOR A BUMPY RIDE

See also road rage

There are some roads that seem more like amusement park rides rather than pave-ment. Your car rises and falls with a ferocity that threatens to puncture your tires and shake your fillings lose. One of the main causes of potholes is

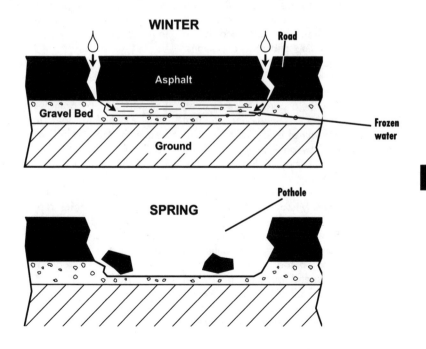

WINTER

Road

Asphalt

Gravel Bed

Frozen water

Ground

SPRING

Pothole

P

water. When it is a liquid, water seeps into little cracks in the cement. Then, on cold days, it freezes. When water freezes it expands. This makes the cracks bigger. When the ice melts and takes up less space, it leaves a gap in the concrete and bits fall in. A pothole is created.

Another cause of potholes is politics. Potholes are seen most frequently in areas where state highway departments have less money than necessary to keep roads in repair. The Environmental Working Group, a content provider for public interest groups, analyzed Department of Transportation records on spending and road conditions. They found that more than half of the nation's urban highways are in fair to poor condition. About 26 percent are in need of repair. They conclude that one out of every 15 miles traveled by an American driver is on a potted, rutted road. This, they say, is the equivalent of a trip from New York City to St. Louis, Missouri on bad roads.

State highway departments spend about $1.2 billion a year on road repair, but drivers spend four times more than that, $4.8 billion a year, on repairing damage to their cars caused by potholes and other poor road conditions—shocks, suspension and tires. If you live in Arkansas, Mississippi, Virginia, North Carolina or South Carolina, you're probably no stranger to potholes. These states score highest on the "Pothole Index." That is, they have the highest percentage of highway in poor or mediocre condition while spending the least on highway repair per mile. The large metropolitan areas with the highest pothole indexes are Norfolk, Virginia; Charlotte, North Carolina; Orlando, Florida and Richmond, Virginia. If you live in one of these areas, you may want to invest in cushioned seats.

While we're on the subject, here's a pothole trivia question: Which Beatles song was partially inspired by potholes? A: "A Day in the Life." John Lennon frequently took lyrical inspiration from his daily newspaper. The "4,000 holes in Blackburn, Lancashire" came from a report of the Blackburn City Council survey of road holes reported in the Daily Mail, January 17, 1967. The survey found that there was one twenty-sixth of a hole in the road for each Blackburn resident.

POWERPOINTIZATION OF THE NATION

See also computers, improvements that make things worse

Um, good afternoon. Just a minute while I get my laptop plugged in. OK.

POWERPOINT PET PEEVE ARTICLE
Laura Lee

Good afternoon. Oh, I said that. Anyway, today I'm here to talk about how the nation has become dependent on PowerPoint presentation software for business communications and lectures.

WHY IS POWERPOINT EVERYWHERE?
• Bullet Points and Multi-modal communication and learning
• History of PowerPoint
• Ubiquity of Microsoft Office

Bullet Points and Repetition: The creators of PowerPoint did not invent bullet points, colorful slides or repetitive speech. We can thank researchers of the 1960s and 1970s for that. They studied how to convey information for best retention and concluded the most effective teaching method is to give a preview of what you're about to say, present a question that you are going to answer in the text or speech, provide the informa-

PowerPoint Pet Peeves
• Why is PowerPoint everywhere?
• What's so annoying about PowerPoint use?

P

tion as briefly as possible, and then go back over what you just said. It helps if you use lots of visual aids.

These studies formed the basis for modern textbooks with pictures, review questions and summaries and is also the underlying basis of PowerPoint.

History of PowerPoint: In 1985, a company called Forethought created PowerPoint for Apple's Macintosh. Two years later, Microsoft bought the company for $14 million. By 1994 PowerPoint was the most commonly used presentation software.

WHAT'S SO ANNOYING ABOUT POWERPOINT USE?
• Too Much of a Good Thing
• Over Dependence
• Lack of Creativity, Eloquence

Too Much of a Good Thing: The reason color slides worked as visual aids in the past was that they were sufficiently rare to command the viewer's attention. When slides were a luxury, chances were they conveyed important information. Today's digitized color "slides" often display nothing but headers. When the presentation becomes routine, it is easy to ignore.

Over dependence: PowerPoint becomes annoying when users lose the ability to present their ideas in any other fashion. As venture capitalist Steve Jurvetson told *USA Today:* "I've seen people who get in a mental rut and are unable to write anything other than bullet point lists."

Lack of Creativity, Eloquence: The result, many critics say, is a loss of the art of speaking. Peter Norvig of the NASA Ames Research Center illustrated this by putting Lincoln's Gettysburg Address into PowerPoint form and posting it on the Web. "I started up PowerPoint and let the Autocontent Wizard help me create a new presentation," he writes. "I selected the Company Meeting (Online) template and figured from there I'd be creative in adding bad design wherever possible. I was surprised that the Autocontent Wizard had anticipated my desires so well that I had to make very few changes." If you'd like to see how the famous piece of oratory fares when reduced to bullet points visit http://www.norvig.com/ Gettysburg/sld001.htm.

In conclusion... Oh. It looks like my laptop spontaneously rebooted...

ROAD RAGE AND ROAD RUDENESS

ROAD RAGE AND ROAD RUDENESS

See also caught in traffic, parking lot wars, slow drivers in the fast lane

By day he's a mild-mannered CPA, well-liked by all. Get him behind the wheel and it's a different story. He rides your bumper like one of the villains on an episode of *Speed Racer.* He nearly runs you off the road and pulls into your lane with only millimeters to spare. As he passes, he flashes you a one-finger salute. You half expect to see him release an oil slick as he speeds away. You could laugh it all off, but you're behind the wheel too. Visions of shooting him off the road with laser death rays dance through your head.

Something about driving brings out the worst in people. A recent national study of driving behavior by a Michigan firm showed that almost 80 percent of drivers are angry most of the time while driving. Drivers said their blood boiled at everything from looking for a parking space to having to merge when a highway narrows.

Researchers at Trinity College, Dublin, chalk it up to 'de-individualization.' That is, people see the traffic offender as a vehicle rather than as a person. Psychologists Leon James and Diane Nahl have spent two decades studying aggressive driving. "You're protected in your vehicle," Nahl said. "There's a sense of isolation—the metal dome around you and the power of the engine. It gives you a false sense of security that you can basically do whatever you want without risk."

Anger on the roadways also comes when drivers feel they are no longer in control, says E. Scott Geller, a psychology professor at Virginia Polytechnic Institute. "You've been controlling me all day long in the workplace, punching my clock," he said in a recent interview. "Now I'm in my car, I have this need to feel free, in control." So you speed and tailgate and feel justified in doing so.

Aggressive driving is not limited to American society; in fact, the term "road rage" was coined in England. Nor is it new. Researchers have uncovered accounts of "buggy rage" and they suspect there was probably "chariot rage" as well. That said, experts agree aggressive driving is on the rise. Every year it causes 400,000 accidents, injuring or killing 1,500 people. Police departments nationwide have responded with stricter laws against aggressive driving. Nahl suggests a different approach—personal responsibility. "People don't realize that they are the aggressive drivers," she said. "They always think it's the other people. You need to learn methods of coping because it's very easy to go from annoyance to anger to rage. The best overall solution is to practice civility and become good at it. Driving is a group activity, not an individual activity. It requires teamwork."

80 percent of drivers are angry most of the time

Fist, sometimes one-finger salute

Car offers false sense of security and protection

R

SLOW DRIVERS THROUGH **STUPID WARNING LABELS**

SLOW DRIVERS
IN THE FAST LANE

See also caught in traffic, parking lot wars, road rage

The morning commute is the setting for any number of aggravations—bottle necks, drivers who cut you off only to stop for a turn, trucks that splatter mud all over your windshield.

But what do drivers hate more than anything else?

According to Dr. Diane Nahl, a psychologist who specializes in our behavior on the roads, in two decades of research, her surveys have revealed that the most aggravating culprit is

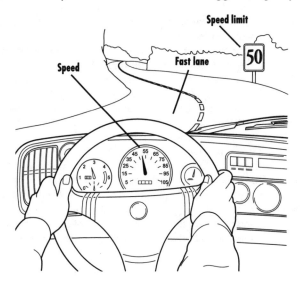

S

"the passive-aggressive driver who's going the speed limit in the fast lane."

"When someone does that you feel like you're being thwarted," she says. "You're being forced to go a speed you don't want to go, and they're in your way. It's a feeling of making people be good and teaching them a lesson. It's all about making sure you're getting what you need and want. If others aren't getting what they need and want that's their problem."

"Impeding the flow of traffic" by driving slowly in the passing lane is an offense in most states, but it is not highly enforced.

If you want to get the slow driver out of your way, retired New York State Trooper James M. Eagan says, the best way is to quickly flash your headlights.

"Do this when you are about three to four truck lengths behind him," he writes in his book *A Speeder's Guide to Avoiding Tickets: The Essential Manual for Life in the Fast Lane.* If you wait too long, he says, the offending driver may consider you a tailgater and "punish" you by slowing down or refusing to budge.

"Aggressive drivers want minimum speed limits, not maximum," wrote traffic psychology researchers Dr. Leon James and Dr. Diane Nahl in their book *Road Rage and Aggressive Driving.* "Rushing mania is one of the most common driving obsessions…[It] has two complementary elements. One is an extraordinary need to avoid slowing down. The other is the consequent anger against anyone who causes a slow down."

James believes tailgating is a symptom of a larger problem—a cultural trend to respond to annoyances with anger. "People feel entitled in public places," he says. "If anyone stands in the way I have the right to be angry—maybe retaliate. Take a look at the post office, people stand in line, but what are they thinking? We've had students write down their thoughts and feelings and we get an idea that people carry on, cognitively, a constant verbal attack and criticism of others."

In any case, tailgating won't get you there any faster. Tailgaters actually get blocked in more often than other drivers because they can't anticipate problems ahead and select the best lane.

SNORING

He snores, you say. That doesn't really begin to describe it. Your bed partner's nose produces a rumbling that frightens small children... in the next time zone. A long, fierce vibration followed by a teasing pause and a tense wait. You know another snort is coming.

Sari Zayed of Davis, California, made headlines in 1994 when a city noise enforcement officer issued Zayed a $50 citation at 1:30 in the morning after a neighbor complained her snoring kept him awake at night. Zayed got the last laugh. She sued for $24,500 for stress, lost wages and emotional strain and settled out of court for $13,500.

Snorers aren't trying to keep others awake at night. Most of the time, they don't even know they snore—they are, after all, unconscious at the time. Some anthropologists have suggested that snoring is a primitive way of keeping beasts away at night. Ear, nose and throat doctors take a different view.

When you breathe, you create a negative pressure to suck in air. When you sleep, the soft tissues in the back of your mouth and throat—the soft palate, tonsils, adenoids and uvula (that little thing that hangs down)—

Uvula

The sound of snoring can exceed 55 decibels

S

relax and prevent air from flowing freely. You reflexively try to pull in air quickly, creating turbulence. As many as 90 million Americans snore, according to the National Sleep Foundation. The biggest snorers are middle-aged men (about half of them snore) and overweight people. If you know a man with a neck size over 16 inches, there is a good chance he's a heavy snorer. Otolaryngologist Kent Wilson of the University of Minnesota at Minneapolis hung a microphone over 1,139 people as they slept and found that some snores topped 55 decibels, about the volume of rush hour traffic.

Doctors take snoring seriously. The most serious form is sleep apnea, in which the sleeper actually stops breathing for periods of at least 10 seconds, hundreds of times a night. During as much as half their sleep time, patients with sleep apnea may show below-average concentrations of oxygen in their blood. A lack of oxygen can cause the heart to pump harder and over time can contribute to high blood pressure.

During REM sleep, the brain sends out an inhibitor that basically paralyzes the body, presumably to keep you from acting out vivid dreams. When a sleep apnea sufferer's breathing is cut off, the body rouses itself with a jolt of adrenaline. Breathing resumes, the person falls back to sleep and the whole thing starts again. These "micro-arousals" can happen as many as 600 times a night, disrupting a snorer's sleep cycle. Studies have linked their apnea induced sleepiness to an increase in car accidents. A study by the Mayo Clinic also shows that spouses of heavy snorerst lose an average of one hour's sleep a night.

People have been trying to develop snoring cures as far back as the American Revolution when soldiers sewed small cannonballs into pockets on the back of the snoring-offenders' uniforms so they would not roll onto their backs. Today, more than 300 anti-snoring devices are registered with the U.S. Patent and Trademark Office.

To reduce your nighttime noise making, doctors suggest losing weight, avoiding alcohol within three hours before you go to sleep and ironically, getting enough sleep. If that doesn't work, consult a physician. There are a number of things they can try, such as breathing masks, mouthpieces and surgery.

SONG STUCK IN YOUR HEAD, OR CEREBRUM ANNOYING REFLUX ACTION

Everyone has had the experience of having an annoyingly catchy, and often hated, song lodged firmly in the mind. The Germans use the word *Ohrwurm*, which translates to 'earworm' or 'earwig,' for tunes that invade the consciousness. "You can't get rid of earworms," reader Tony Shelbroune wrote

...you do the Hokey Pokey and you turn yourself around...

Song running through head

Dr. Harvey Master
speaking tonight
"The Theory of
Quantum Physics"

S

in a letter to London's *Independent*. "But you can make them breed. There is real satisfaction in getting a normally musically sophisticated colleague whistling 'Una Paloma Blanca.'"

Dr. Judith Rappaport, who specializes in treating victims of Obsessive-Compulsive Disorder, described an extreme case to *People* magazine. The man heard the same six fiddle notes for 31 years. "When he finally admitted it to his wife, she wept with joy because she had thought that he just wasn't interested in listening to her, she said." In 2000, an American man had surgery of the right lateral temporal cortex to stop the song "Owner of a Lonely Heart" by Yes from playing over and over in his mind.

Not even animals are immune. A group of scientists at the University of Sydney in Australia studied humpback whale song from 1995 to 1998. They found that a song that was at first sung only by two males quickly spread. By the end of 1997 the entire group had adopted it.

There is, apparently, some kind of neurological underpinning in all this. Songs can be triggered by stimulating an area in the brain that processes sound patterns. Researchers have apparently not devoted a great deal of serious study to earworms, however. "I don't know any research in that area," said Dr. Rebecca Mercuri, an expert in the field of psychoacoustics, "but one would think it would be too annoying to research."

What makes the phenomenon so aggravating is that you are much more likely to find yourself humming "Achy Breaky Heart" than Mozart. "You remember the unusual, the odd and the awful particularly well," Rebecca Rupp, the author of several books on memory and learning, told the *Toledo Blade*. "It's not necessarily praiseworthy, but it's the way memory works."

Jim Nayder, host of *The Annoying Music Show*, calls it "Cerebrum annoying reflux action." When he has a particularly odious melody lodged in his gray matter, he solves the problem by seeking out an even more annoying song. All together now: "Babe, I got you, babe...."

SOUR MILK

Nothing spoils your morning like casually pouring milk on your cereal and taking a big bite only to discover—eee-wwww—the milk is off.

Sour milk is fermented milk. Milk is made up of fat, proteins and sugars. It is actually between 12 and 13 percent solid, more solid than many vegetables. The composition of the milk is influenced by the breed and age of the specific cow and when the milk was drawn. The last milk drawn at each milking is richest in fat. The same food stuffs that are useful to humans are a feast for bacteria.

When the milk comes out of the cow, it is actually bacteria-free.

HOW MILK BECOMES SOUR

Carton of fresh milk is opened. → Bacteria get into the milk. → Time passes. →

→ Bacteria feast on lactose and convert it to lactic acid. → Milk in carton becomes spoiled.

S

Once the air gets to it, the bacteria begin their colonization. Pasteurization—heating milk to 161 F for 15 seconds—kills the kinds of bacteria that might result in disease, but a few harmless spoilage bacteria remain behind. As long as the carton or jug remains unopened, few new bacteria can get in to the liquid. Thus, an unopened container lasts longer than one that is opened. The spoilage bacteria do not do well in very low temperatures, which is why milk must be refrigerated. It should be kept at a temperature below 40 F. At that temperature, it should last about 14 days.

During those two weeks, the spoilage bacteria feast on the milk sugar, or lactose. They convert the lactose into lactic acid through a fermentation process. When there is enough lactic acid, the milk gains that distinctive sour smell and odd taste. Skim milk tends to stay fresh longer than whole milk because whole milk has more lactose. If you have any of your grandmother's recipes, you may have a few that call for "sour milk." The acid in the sour milk would react with baking soda to create bubbles of carbon dioxide that make baked goods rise.

Such recipes pre-date pasteurization. These days, milk that has had time to go sour probably has had time to attract and grow some unhealthy spoilage bacteria as well. Instead of using sour milk, substitute buttermilk in those recipes for the same effect.

Curdling of milk is caused by protein called casein. It is normally dispersed throughout the fluid of the milk. When the milk has aged as long as it apparently does in your refrigerator, the curds (solid) separate from the whey (liquid).

As for those "sell by" dates on milk—milk will not instantly expire on that day. Milk containers are stamped with a date that is 14 days from the time the milk was pasteurized and packed. It takes about two days for milk to get from the cow to the store. There it is refrigerated at 40 degrees or less. It should then last another week past the "expiration date" assuming you also keep it refrigerated.

SPEEDING TICKETS

See also road rage, slow drivers in the fast lane

Little can dampen your mood as quickly as watching the police car you zoomed past pull out of the median and turn on the blue strobe lights. Then there's the question: "Do you know how fast you were going?"

Is there a right answer to that question? If you say "Yes, I was going 85," you admit you were speeding. If you say, "I was going the speed limit," you

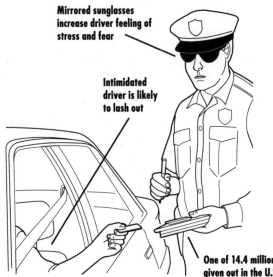

Mirrored sunglasses increase driver feeling of stress and fear

Intimidated driver is likely to lash out

One of 14.4 million speeding tickets given out in the U.S. each year

annoy the officer because you both know that's a lie.

If you want to avoid getting a ticket, James M. Eagen, a retired New York State Trooper and author of the book *A Speeder's Guide to Avoiding Tickets*, suggests you put the ball back in the policeman's court. "Your best bet is to try a comment like, 'I just wasn't paying attention like I should have officer, how fast was I going?'"

Most of us are more likely to talk ourselves into tickets than out of them. To increase your chances of driving off with a warning, Eagen says you should always try to reduce the policeman's fear and feed his ego. Try to engage him in conversation so he sees you as a human being and don't do anything to challenge his authority.

The problem is that everything about a speeding stop is calculated to increase your fear and deflate your ego. A study by the Canadian Mounties has shown that if the officer is wearing mirrored sunglasses your feelings of stress and fear rise. You're likely to perceive of the cop as more aggressive and less courteous than if you could see his eyes. If he is wearing a visible holstered gun, your anger

and fear rises even more. Frightened, angry drivers are more likely to mouth off or even pull out a weapon. If you want to avoid that ticket, it's your job to break the vicious cycle.

Don't apologize or promise not to speed again, Eagen says, the officer lives in the same world as the rest of us and he knows just about everyone speeds. He doesn't believe you are sorry, and he doesn't believe you won't do it again.

"The members of the hierarchy do not want you to slow down," he writes. "Despite their public service announcements to the contrary, they want you to speed so you can get a ticket."

In 1999, police wrote an estimated 14.4 million speeding tickets in this country. Some cities generate as much as 75 percent of their revenue from traffic enforcement. South Carolina leads the nation with 279,000 tickets followed by North Carolina with 265,000 and Virginia with 246,000.

As to that age-old question, "what is the real speed limit?" Eagen says most officers will not stop a driver who is going 10–20 miles over the limit.

STANDING TOO CLOSE

See also armrest wars, inefficient sidewalk pass, legroom, office cubicles, too much perfume

You're in a public place and a strange woman comes up to you and engages you in conversation. As she speaks, you become nervous and stiff. She is standing about a step closer than you want her to be. You try to back away without being obvious, and a strange dance begins. During the course of the conversation you move halfway across the room, but she always ends up just a little bit closer than you want her to be. By all accounts, she is trying to be pleasant and social, and yet you can't wait for her to go away. Why? She has invaded your personal space.

According to Edward T. Hall, a pioneering researcher in the field of proxemics—the study of our use of space—we set our boundaries by the time we reach the age of 12. Different cultures have different boundaries, but no culture is without its own sense of space. Every person, indeed, every animal, is surrounded by an invisible egg-shaped field. The reason it is not a circle is that we will let people come in closer from the front than from behind.

In American culture there are four distinctive spatial zones. The closest extends outwards about 18 inches. Only those who are the most intimate, lovers or parents with children, are allowed within the boundary. The next zone, reserved for close friends, extends from 18 inches to 4 feet. Coworkers and casual acquaintances are expected to remain at a distance of 4 feet to 10 feet. Strangers are permitted from 10 to 25 feet. In American culture, the distance between an audience and a podium is generally about 30 feet. When we encounter people with a different sense of personal space, such as people who were raised in different cultures, it makes us uncomfortable, irritable and in extreme cases, physically ill.

When most people lived in rural areas or on farms, personal space was not a pressing issue. It has been estimated that in the medieval world the average person saw one hundred other people in the course of a *lifetime*. As the Industrial Revolution swept the world and crowded people into cities, we developed a variety of methods of coping with the constant infringement on our space. We have a set of unwritten rules about how close to stand and when to acknowledge others. We create boundaries by placing coats or books on the seat beside us. In elevators, we face forward and rarely make eye

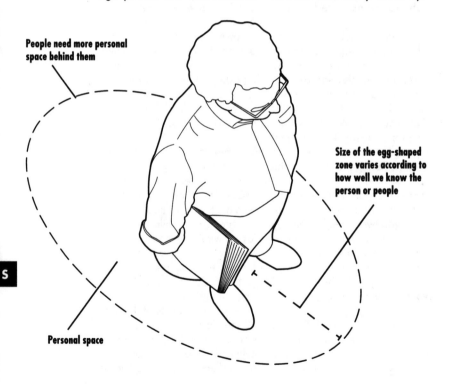

People need more personal space behind them

Size of the egg-shaped zone varies according to how well we know the person or people

Personal space

contact. Even though no one taught you in so many words, as a North American or Northern European, you know that you can ignore a person standing 10 feet away, but once he gets to 8 feet, it is time to smile or say hello.

When space is limited, we try to preserve an internal sense of space by shutting ourselves off from others. If we cannot get the people out of our space, we do our best to pretend they are not people. This is easily observed in commuter trains, subways and airplanes. The legal capacity of a New York subway train allows 20 cubic feet of space per person, but the passengers have to stand or sit closer to each other when using handrails. The Tokyo subway crowds passengers into 5 cubic feet or less.

Passengers try to create their own space by reading books or magazines or looking out the window. If they can't, they will often look down towards their feet and generally avoid eye contact with the people in the surrounding seats. The exercise is stressful and exhausting. Researchers have found that after an hour's ride on a crowded Japanese commuter train, it takes about an hour and a half for a commuter to completely get over the strain and fatigue.

Robert Sommer, a psychologist at the University of California-Davis, wrote an entire book, *Personal Space,* on how people react when we break such rules. He conducted his research by going into libraries and sitting too close to people.

"They begin by tapping their toes," he says. "They pull at their hair. They get completely rigid. It may not trigger a full-blown schizophrenic episode, but it's clearly not good for your health."

STUPID WARNING LABELS

Found on the wrapper of a 7-11 sandwich: "Remove toothpick before eating."

How stupid do product makers think we are? Very, very stupid. If there is an absolutely wrong way to use a product, some hapless American will surely find it. Thanks to the prevalence of TV commercials and advertising the services of personal injury lawyers, even the most common-sense-challenged citizen is savvy enough to sue.

In 1991, the U.S. was home to 70 percent of the world's lawyers, and they are busy. In 1960, Americans filed fewer than 100,000 lawsuits in Federal courts. In 1990 that number had risen to 250,000. Litigation adds an estimated 2.5 percent to the average cost of a new product in America, more if it is related to medicine, health or technology. One research group

reports that court costs, awards and lost time cost the economy $132 billion in 1991 alone.

Some analysts say the problem is that cases are decided by people who can't get out of jury duty. "Juries are made up of people who themselves do not want to take responsibility," a 1998 Ardell Wellness Report said. "Thus, they may identify with these hapless plaintiffs."

To protect themselves, manufacturers print up warnings that insult our intelligence at every turn. Some real examples: on a pair of bicycle shin guards: "Shin pads cannot protect any part of the body they do not cover"; on an industrial wood router: "This product not intended for use as a dental drill or in medical applications"; on bagged peanuts: "Caution-remove shell before consuming nutmeats"; on the instruction plate of an elevator: "May be operated only where installed"; on Jolly Rancher candies: "Warning: Small objects like hard candies may become inadvertently lodged in the throat"; on a Sears hair dryer: "Do not use while sleeping"; on the Windows 98 operating system "Do not make illegal copies of this disc"; and, of course, there is the McDonald's coffee warning: "Caution: Hot."

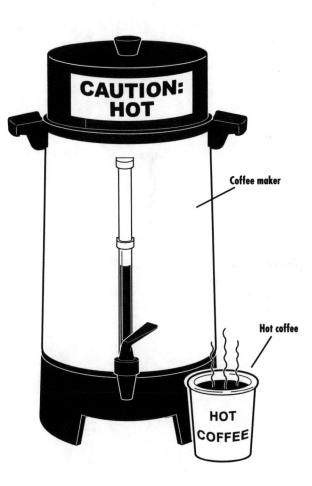

CAUTION: HOT

Coffee maker

Hot coffee

HOT COFFEE

T

TELEMARKETING THROUGH **TV: ALWAYS ON**

TELEMARKETING

See improvements that make things worse

The phone rings in the middle of dinner. "Hello?" A moment passes. You hear a cacophony of voices in the background.

"Hello?" You repeat. "Hello Mr. Smith, I'm calling regarding your Citibank card. Because you are such a valued customer..."

No one knows exactly who first had the idea to pick up a

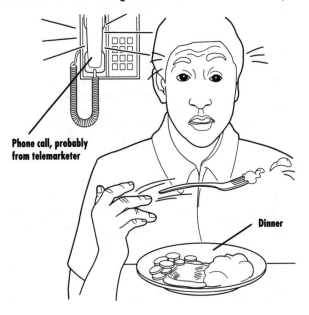

Phone call, probably from telemarketer

Dinner

phone and start selling. It simply evolved as a logical next step from the door-to-door salesman. A 1927 telephone sales manual published by the Bell Telephone Company of Pennsylvania touted the potential of the technology for sales: "The telephone provides the simplest, most effective and most economical means of increasing the number of contacts between salesman and buyer," it said.

"Telephone marketing has been going on for quite some time," says Kevin Brosnahan of American Teleservices Association (ATA), "but true telemarketing had its beginnings in the late 1970s/early 1980s, when telephone technology really began to take off. Before that, most telephone marketing consisted of appointment-setting."

Not so any more. Thanks to computer technology, telemarketing has become highly efficient, and highly profitable. Most telemarketing organizations, about 75 percent, use predictive dialing systems. With predictive dialing, the computer places the call. If the line is busy or if no one picks up, it dials another number. If you do pick up, it connects the call to an operator. This is why you often hear a tell-tale delay when you pick

up the phone. (The good news is, it does give you an opportunity to hang up. Answer to a delay accented by the sound of many other people talking in the background—good chance it's not a personal call.)

If it seems you have been getting more hang-up calls than in the past, you can blame this on predictive dialing as well. The computers dial numbers even when all the operators are busy. With busy signals and non-answers, odds are that at least one operator will have completed a call (or had someone slam the phone down) by the time the machine connects. Sometimes, though, the computer dials a number, you pick up, and there are no operators available. The machine hangs up on you. Companies can set the percentage of hang-up calls a system allows, it is called the abandonment rate. The higher the rate, the more hang-ups.

The Direct Marketing Association recommends an abandonment rate of no higher than 5 percent, but some telemarketers are setting the abandonment rate as high as 40 percent. They want the phones to be constantly dialing. When operators have to dial manually, they spend only 15 minutes out of an hour selling according to a spokesperson for EIS International, which makes predictive dialing systems. With the aid of the system, they can increase talk time up to 45 minutes an hour. Productivity has been known to increase 200–300 percent.

In 1998, *USA Today* reported that Americans get about 10 billion telemarketing calls a year. We hate them. We consider them an invasion of our privacy and time. Paul Jerome Croche, an associate professor in the Department of American Studies at Stetson University, believes telemarketing contributes to an overall rudeness in society.

"Manners have become the clipped codes of smooth market relations," he wrote in *The Public Perspective*. "Phone solicitations begun with a cheerful first-name greeting are eminently mannerly, but mask a bald pitch for money... It is more tempting to act without manners... because [manners] are used so often to persuade against one's will."

Certainly we're not on our best behavior when dealing with telemarketers. We hang up on them. We scream at them and plot revenge against them. The operators making the calls usually earn a dollar or two above minimum wage. They talk to up to 20 people an hour and suffer repeated abuse and rejection. Most employees don't stay long. It is estimated that one in ten quits within the first month.

With that kind of ill will, why do they call? In 1994, telemarketing generated $339 billion in sales. In 1999, it had jumped to $538 billion. The Direct Marketing Association predicts that sales will skyrocket to more than $811 billion by 2004. Forget the loud whistles, the caller ID and the do not call lists—if everyone stopped taking advantage of incredible one-time-only offers over the telephone, telemarketers wouldn't make any money and they'd stop calling.

T

TOAST ALWAYS LANDS BUTTER SIDE DOWN

Why is it that if you drop a piece of toast, chances are, it will land with the butter side down? Some scientists say this is not true. According to the makers of a BBC science program, *Q.E.D.*, the reason we believe the toast is apt to land on the buttery side is that we remember all the times it lands badly and forget the times it lands well. Physicist Robert Matthews set out to prove them wrong. "The experiments carried out by the programme were dynamically inappropriate," he wrote in the *European Journal of Physics*, "in that they consisted of people simply tossing buttered bread into the air."

Matthews tested his theory by dropping pieces of buttered toast over the side of a table. When that got "sort of messy" he switched to toast-sized pieces of wood. He discovered that toast does, in fact, tend to land butter side down. It has nothing to do with the weight of the butter. It has to do with gravitational torque and the height of the average table.

Once the toast slides off the edge of the plate, it starts to flip, but the gravitation torque is not sufficient enough to right the toast again before it hits the floor. So, if you sense your toast is about to take a tumble, Matthews suggests giving it a swipe with your hand to increase its speed at take off. If you don't possess the requisite skill to save your bread in this manner, he includes a few more entertaining methods of preventing a butter-side-down mishap, including eating tiny squares of toast, buttering the underside or "tying the toast to a cat, which of course knows how to get right-side up during a fall."

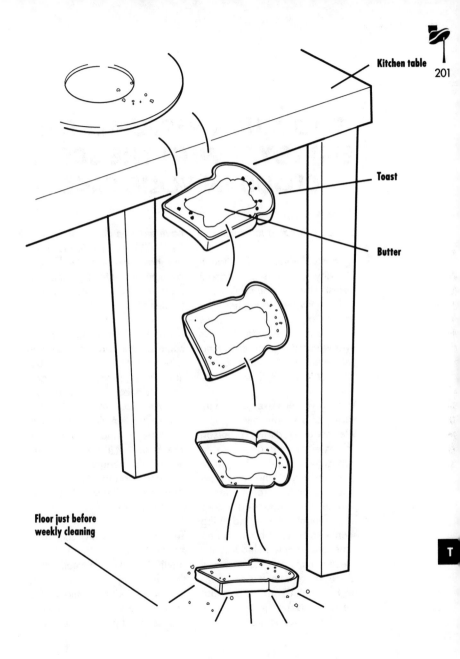

Kitchen table

Toast

Butter

Floor just before
weekly cleaning

T

TOO MUCH PERFUME: THE EMPLOYEE WITH THE SCENT CLOUD IN YOUR FACE

See also standing too close

Your colleague is intelligent, witty and has a pleasant personality, but you can't stand to be anywhere near her. The gallons of cologne she bathes in make you sneeze, make your eyes water and generally offend your nose. It's perfume to her, it's odor to you.

Your coworker's excess is an invasion of your personal space. We mentally allow a person about eight feet of space in public places. If their fragrance wafts past that line, it is now in our space. In recent years, people with offended noses have fought back by adopting scent-free policies banning perfume and scented deodorants. These actions are most common at schools and universities. Supporters of the zones argue that the smell is not just intrusive, but dangerous to people who

have multiple chemical sensitivity (MCS). Victims of the disorder have become overloaded by environmental chemicals so their immune systems overreact to them.

MCS is controversial. While some doctors are now specializing in its treatment, others believe it is psychosomatic, and some doubt it exists at all. The American Medical Association, The American Academy of Allergy and Immunology, The Board of the International Society of Regulatory Toxicology and Pharmacology and the American College of Physicians don't recognize it.

The problem with scent-free zones is that they tend to ban anything that has a smell rather than focusing on the chemicals themselves, which would tend to support the idea that it is more a question of personal space invasion than a concern over allergic reactions. You perceive smell when your nose senses traces of chemicals in the air and it conveys the message to the brain. The brain lets you know if the fragrance is pleasant or unpleasant. It doesn't always correspond to the danger level of the chemical. Natural gas is odorless, new-mown grass is fragrant.

The $42 billion perfume industry produces at least 100 new scents each year. The simplest fragrance might have up to 100 different ingredients. More complex—and more expensive scents—can have several hundred. It is estimated that there are between 5,000 and 6,000 commercially produced fragrances in the world.

Many in the environmental movement are specific in their grievances and want only chemically synthesized perfumes banned. Certain perfume ingredients, they say, are toxic and cause cancer.

Issues of health aside, there are good reasons why you might not like a specific perfume and why you feel so strongly about it. The sensory nerves in the nose are connected to the temporal lobe of the brain where memory is stored, and are closely tied to the limbic region, which is re-

Average perceived allowable distance for perfume to carry

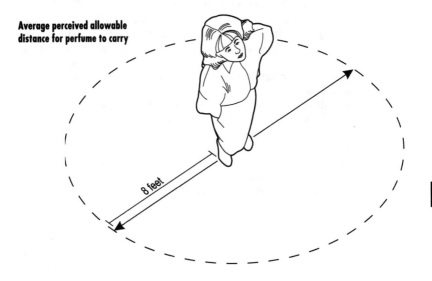

8 feet

sponsible for the most basic impulses—appetite, fear and sex. Whatever you feel about that perfume, you're going to have strong emotions about it.

In fact, scientists have recently discovered that some of the information we get from the nose does not register in the brain as smell at all but directly as emotion. Researchers from the University of Utah discovered the vermeronasal organ in humans, a pair of pits in the nostrils that signal the brain when they detect certain substances. When these organs were signaling, the subjects were not consciously aware of a smell but reported a feeling of well-being. So when you smell that perfume, you may well be reacting at a level you cannot consciously appreciate.

Scientists no longer believe there is a single human "pheromone" that drives members of the opposite sex wild. Yet scent may play a bigger role in attraction than was previously believed and interestingly, it is related not to sex hormones but to the immune system. Whenever the body is invaded by an alien body (a virus, bacteria, an implanted organ) the immune system attaches protein identifiers to it and creates antibodies specifically designed to combat it. A segment of our DNA, the major histocompalibity complex (MHC), "remembers" this information and codes for it.

Researchers discovered that women rate the smells of men whose MHC profiles were different from their own, sexier than those whose MHC codes were similar. They theorize that we sniff out mates, whose immunities are different from our own, so as to produce stronger, healthier babies—the kids would be born with resistance to more diseases. A study by evolutionary ecologists Manfred Millinsky and Claus Wedekind found that participants with the same MHC types tended to prefer similar scents for their own use, but disliked the idea of the smells on a partner. They concluded that people select a perfume that amplifies the natural signal produced by their immune system so it accentuates the natural odor. If you don't like your coworker's perfume, blame it on evolution.

TV: ALWAYS ON

See also annoying commercials, blaring commercials, free time? what free time?

You go to a friend's house to visit. You're a TV-on, TV-off kind of person. Your friend, on the other hand, sees her television as nothing more than a glowing, sound-producing decoration in the corner. It's always on, but it's so ubiquitous that it commands little attention. Since the TV is on, you're trying to watch it. Why is she interrupting all the time? How rude! She, meanwhile, is wondering why you came all this way if you just want to watch the TV. You seem too distracted to talk. How rude!

Americans say that TV is the least necessary part of their lives, yet they devote more time to it than to any other leisure activity. They estimate that they have less than 20 hours of free time a week, yet they also report watching 21 hours of TV a week.

"Virtually all the added 'leisure' gained over the last 30 years has been spent on the couch in front of the tube," wrote Robert D. Putnam in his foreword to *Time for Life: The Surprising Ways Americans Use Their Time.* "The increase in TV-watching has cut into the time we have allocated to almost everything else in our lives—but most especially to activities outside the home."

Studies in 1978 and 1986 both showed that television viewing reduced participation in community activities like clubs, parties, dances and sports. A 1990 study reported that heavy TV viewers felt less happy, friendly and positive than light viewers. The researchers came to no conclusion as to whether heavy

T

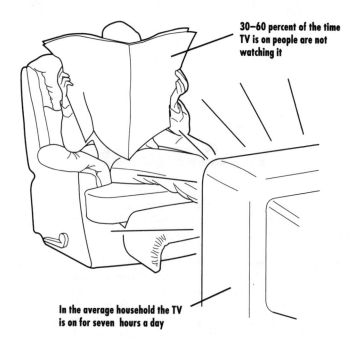

30–60 percent of the time TV is on people are not watching it

In the average household the TV is on for seven hours a day

television viewing was a symptom of ennui or its cause.

As we devote more time to television, we seem to appreciate it less. It becomes more habit than entertainment. The fact that we spend increasing portions of our leisure doing an activity we only marginally enjoy contributes to our sense of lost time.

In many homes, television is a constant companion. Background noise. Much of the time, television "viewers" are really not viewers at all. They're listeners, or "walk-past"-ers.

"Today, radio is almost exclusively a secondary activity, something we listen to while doing something else," wrote *Time for Life* authors John P. Robinson and Geoffrey Godbey. "Television is beginning to go the same way as radio—at least one quarter of television viewing is combined with other activities."

Depending on whose study you believe, 30–60 percent of the

time the television is on you're not actually watching. Nielsen, the folks who track TV viewing, find that on most days in the average home, television sets are physically on and tuned to one channel or another for about seven hours. They estimate the average American actually watches about four hours a day.

When the TV is on, boys and men tend to look more than women and girls. Not surprisingly, boys pay more attention to programs with animation and action.

Children begin "watching" TV in infancy, when parents put them in front of the box to quiet them down. Videotapes of children show that while they watch TV, they also play, eat, do homework and talk. Television becomes easy to ignore.

One study demonstrated that Israeli children learn more from educational television than their American counterparts. The two groups learned equally well when they received information in print, but Americans are so used to tuning out television that they pay less attention to the content.

A group called TV-Free America sponsors a national TV Turn-Off Week. They say that TV-free families have about an hour of meaningful conversation per day compared with a national average of 38 minutes per week and that 80 percent of no-TV households surveyed said their marriages were stronger because they had more time for each other. You can read more about their campaign on their Web page: http://www.tvturnoff.org/.

There is, of course, a less extreme response than throwing your TV out the window. Experts urge habitual viewers to learn to tell the difference between viewing that actually entertains and informs and viewing that is nothing more than an unsatisfying habit. By limiting viewing to shows you actually look forward to seeing, you can regain some of the time that seems to be slipping away.

So how much should you talk while the TV is on? It depends on the preferences of the people in the room. Maybe you can discuss the issue during a commercial.

T

UNMATCHED SOCKS THROUGH **UNSOLICITED BULK E-MAIL**

UNMATCHED SOCKS

You start out with a drawer full of nice pairs of matched socks. Eventually, the order degrades to the point that you are forced to go to work wearing one argyle and one blue sock. What happened? Where the lost socks go is one of the great mysteries of the universe; but Robert Matthews, a visiting research fellow at Aston University in Birmingham, England,

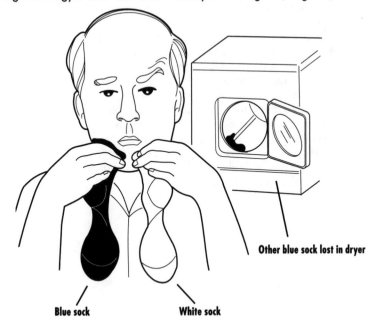

Other blue sock lost in dryer

Blue sock   White sock

has investigated the results. His conclusion, published in *Mathematics Today*, is that if your socks do go missing, you are indeed more likely to end up with unmatched socks than pairs.

Here's how it works, when you lose one sock, it leaves behind its former partner. If you lose another sock, it could be the unmatched one (how great would that be). But there are many more paired socks than single socks, so it is probable that the next sock you lose will not be the matchless one. Because you are less likely to wear and wash the unmatched sock, leaving it safe and sound in the drawer where it is unlikely to be lost, the odds are even greater that the next sock to go will be part of a pair. Using a series of complex sock equations, Matthews concluded that if socks are randomly lost from a drawer initially stocked with 10 complete, but distinct, sock pairs, it is over 100 times more likely that the result will be the worst possible outcome, with 4 complete pairs and 6 odd socks in the drawer, than the best outcome with 7 complete pairs left.

"Drawing two socks at random even from a drawer full of complete pairs is most likely to produce nothing but two odd socks," he writes. "Thus, even if we have judiciously cleared out all the odd socks from our drawer we are still likely to have to rummage through a substantial fraction of the remaining socks before getting just one matching pair." Of course, you increase the chances of pulling out matching socks if you buy only one kind. Matthews thought that was a bit drastic. He decided to limit his own sock purchases to two types, eight pairs of each. He learned, however, that Murphy's Law cannot be broken. After the sock gremlins struck, he returned to the store only to discover that one of the styles had been discontinued.

UNSOLICITED BULK E-MAIL AKA SPAM

See also junk mail, internet flaming

"Incredible Business Offer! This is not spam!" These days many spammers seem to believe that if they say their message is not spam you won't notice it is spam. Oh hey, a message from Bambi inviting me to look at naked, big-breasted teens. It's a good thing this isn't spam or I might be annoyed.

Unsolicited bulk e-mail got its nickname from a sketch on the British television program *Monty Python's Flying Circus* in which everything on the menu came with spam. The in-box of your e-mail program is similar— spam, spam, message from my mom, spam, business correspondence and spam.

Anyone with $50 to spend on software can turn his computer

!	0	▽	From	Subject	Received
			✉ Nosehair.com	FREE gift for sign-on	7:56 AM
			✉ DeLeon.com	Fountain of Youth!	9:29 AM
			✉ STF of America	Save the Funguses	11:28 AM
			✉ Chad and Tina	Dating Secrets Revealed	12:59 PM
	0		✉ Insider Traders	$AVE BIG MONEY!	1:51 PM
			✉ American Hair,Inc	Hair gel that works	2:03 PM
			✉ Sally	Fwd:Fwd:Answer this chain letter or die	2:31 PM
	0		✉ S.O.S.	Sea Slugs Protection	3:29 PM
			✉ Chicken Little	Fwd: WARNING: End of World virus	8:25 PM
	0		✉ Crapper Products	Bulk Toilet Paper Now!	10:32 PM
			✉ SWAK Dating Svc.	I Want You (find out why)	1:55 AM

U

into a spam machine. The software gathers e-mail addresses automatically from Web pages and newsgroups. The question is why anyone would want to. E-mail pitches are more likely to elicit a scalding reply than business. The 2000 WWW User Survey by Georgia Tech's Graphics, Visualization and Usability Center revealed that 91 percent of e-mail users receive spam. More than half, 64 percent, delete it without even opening it. Only 12 percent bother to ask to have their names removed from lists. This is just as well. Internet experts say sending a "remove" request just tells the spammer your email address is active and you will be spammed even more.

Because reputable businesses know they're more likely to cause consumer ill-will than to increase business, most spam comes from less reputable sources. The most common bulk e-mail pitches involve pyramid schemes, "Get Rich Quick" schemes, phone sex and pornographic Web sites, offers for bulk e-mail software, dubious health products, and illegally pirated software.

Then there are the messages that are forwarded by well-intentioned friends: e-mail petitions and virus hoaxes.

People are trying to combat the problem on many fronts—Internet Service Providers follow up on spam complaints by closing offending accounts, there is a variety of proposed legislation on both the state and national levels, and there are filters and software to block unwanted e-mail. To learn the latest on all of these, visit The Coalition Against Unsolicited E-mail at http://www.cauce.org/ or any of a variety of anti-spam Web sites.

The folks at Hormel, makers of the canned meat product, SPAM, aren't thrilled at the association with bulk e-mail, by the way. Yet they have pretty much given up and accepted that we're not going to change our moniker for the annoying messages. Their lawyers, instead, concentrate their energies on making sure people don't capitalize the word "spam" when referring to e-mail and keeping pictures of the meat off of Web pages about Internet spam.

U

VCRS FLASHING THROUGH **VENDING MACHINES**

VCRS FLASHING 12:00...
12:00...

You hold a PhD in astrophysics and can juggle five balls while humming the "Star Spangled Banner," so why can't you set the timer on your freaking VCR? It depends on who you ask. The people who build electronic devices heap the blame on your technophobic shoulders, while others like Donald Norman, author of *The Design of Everyday Things* chalk it up to poor design.

Time magazine estimates that as many as 80 percent of VCR owners have never learned how to set their machines to record a program. A 1990 study showed that one-third of the people who own video cassette recorders never record television shows while they are away from home. A 1992 survey of 1,156 VCR owners showed more than half of them had problems using some of the machine's functions. Such luminaries as Peter Jennings, Katie Couric, Barbara Walters and Tipper Gore admit their VCRs blink 12:00, 12:00. Many people put duct tape over the time so they don't have to watch it flash.

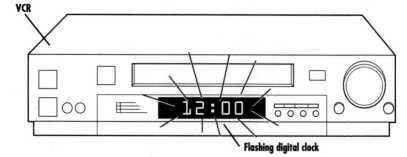

VCR

Flashing digital clock

V

A 1994 study commissioned by Dell Computer determined that 55 percent of Americans suffer some degree of technophobia. Larry Rosen, a psychology professor at California State University, specializes in helping people overcome their fears of technology. He told *Newsday* that technophobia is "an inner problem, not an outer problem... Technophobes say to themselves, 'I can't do this, it's too complicated.'"

But then again, maybe it is too complicated. Donald Norman believes consumers are too fast to blame themselves when the real culprit is bad design. "When we have trouble operating a VCR we have something to blame: the machine's bewildering appearance and the lack of clues to suggest what can be done and how to do it," he writes.

In a well-designed product, the user should know what to do just by looking. Today, he contends, designers love to create machines that look "high tech" where the same buttons have multiple functions. They offer few visual clues as to how they should be operated. If there is only one part that can be operated and only one possible action, no one gets confused. The multiple functions of a VCR, especially when it is linked up to a TV, stereo and cable box, leave the consumer with a dizzying array of options.

If you suspect your own technophobia is to blame, Rosen suggests you try to program the VCR when there is nothing worth watching on TV. This will reduce your stress. Have an even-tempered friend help you.

If you suspect your problem has more to do with poor design, nip the problem in the bud by refusing to buy appliances that you can't comprehend. Manufacturers think consumers prefer attractive and confusing products to less-aesthetic but more usable ones. If you buy incomprehensible machines, they have little incentive to improve the design. Try to program the VCR while you're in the store. If you can't figure it out, buy another model.

VENDING MACHINES SPITTING OUT YOUR DOLLAR

A quarter doesn't go as far as it used to. Fortunately, technology has advanced to the point that machines can read paper money. Unfortunately, technology has not advanced to the point that it can always read paper money. Unless you have been living in a cave for the past five years, chances are, you've had the experience of watching a perfectly good dollar bill slide in and out of a machine accompanied by a distinctive "zzzziipp." Why is it that one machine will accept a wrinkled dollar and another won't? As the computer people say, "it's not a bug, it's a feature."

Vending machines are designed so that their owners can make money. They can't make money if the machine is easily fooled by counterfeit cash and dollar-shaped photocopies. On the other hand, the vendor makes no money if you walk away without buying anything because the machine won't

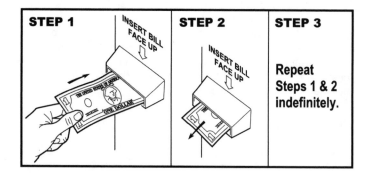

STEP 1	STEP 2	STEP 3
INSERT BILL FACE UP	INSERT BILL FACE UP	Repeat Steps 1 & 2 indefinitely.

take your legal tender. So the manufacturers try to strike a balance between security and accepting mangled money. Coin Acceptors Inc. of St. Louis is one of the leading manufacturers of the devices that read bills. They offer their vendors a choice of three levels of security. Those who put their machines in high traffic areas often opt for high security. A machine in an office might be safe with a lower level of security.

After a machine pulls the paper in, it scans it with light beams. The scanners are so sensitive they can tell what type of ink is used, what color it is, and what type of engravings appear. The highest level of security rejects bills with any imperfections, such as a torn corner. On the other hand, they can also be set so that they will take bills that have been slightly torn, splattered with food, soaked in water or written on with a pen. Even the most forgiving setting, however, can be fooled by a bill that is too crumpled. The folds distort the image on the face. Another possibility is that the machine has not been cleaned regularly and a build up of money grime on the scanners is to blame.

The best advice if a machine rejects your money is to change it in for a new bill. If you can't do that, walk away. Don't try to rock the machine to get a free candy bar—you could get seriously hurt. The Consumer Product Safety Commission reports at least 37 deaths and 113 injuries from toppled machines between 1978 and 1995.

WAITERS, REALLY BAD THROUGH **WHAT IS THE WORD?**

WAITERS, REALLY BAD

See also what did I come in here for?

You're already fidgety and annoyed at having to wait a half hour to get a table at Chez Bob. You even called in a reservation. Chad, your server for this evening, leans on the back of an empty chair as he takes your order. For a moment, you hesitate between ordering the chicken and the fish. "I can come back," he says, and disappears. Ten minutes later he returns, takes your order, but

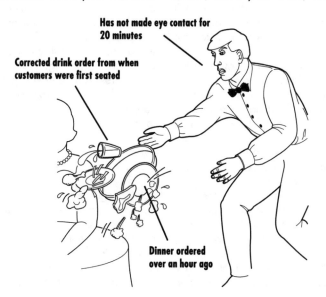

Has not made eye contact for 20 minutes

Corrected drink order from when customers were first seated

Dinner ordered over an hour ago

comes back with the wrong drinks. Once again he sprints away before you can call his attention to the error. Chad steadfastly refuses to make eye contact, and although he passes close to your table three times, he appears to have absolutely no hearing or peripheral vision.

When he brings your meals, you finally have a chance to mention your drink order. He takes your drinks away, promising to return with fresh ones. Time passes. He only returns when you are deep in conversation and interrupts you mid-sentence to ask "How is everything this evening?" "Well, we don't have any drinks!" you snap. He rolls his eyes as if to say, "What a rude customer." By the time Chad returns with the right drinks, three out of four of your guests have finished their meals. Chad starts clearing the plates of all of them, including the one who has not finished. You decide not to risk dessert. Finally, Chad returns with the check and hands it to the only male at the table. He then disappears into a vast waitperson void as his tip dwindles from 15 percent, to 10 percent, to 5 percent... Finally, you take the check to the front of the restaurant and ask whom you can

pay. As you leave, you hear Chad complain loudly that he got stiffed on his tip.

Have waiters gotten worse in the past few years? Probably. A strong economy gave us a boom in restaurants, meanwhile, employees had more options. They could pick and choose their jobs. This led to a shortage of qualified waiters and waitresses. "We joke that pretty soon the chef is going to have to yell: Ok, table number five, come and get your food," said one New Jersey restauranteur.

According to restaurant critic Tim Zagat, women get the worst restaurant service because there is an assumption that women, as a group, do not tip. There is also an assumption that a man at the table is paying. Waiters and waitresses alike tend to put the check down in front of a man, even if a woman is the hostess.

In some countries, waiting tables is considered to be a highly skilled enterprise. There are highly regarded schools in Europe to train waiters. Not so in this country. Here, waiting tables is more often seen as something students and out-of-work actors do. Restaurants don't want to invest in a great deal of training if the employees aren't going to stick around. Waiters who do take pride in their profession are valuable and rare enough that they end up at the top restaurants, not Chez Bob.

According to the National Waiters Association, a good waiter should check on the diner once in the first 90 seconds after the meal is put down on the table. He should then keep the diners in view and pay attention, but should not interrupt with questions like "how is your food?" He should never clear the plates until the slowest diner is through. If the check is delivered to the table, it should be set in the center, not in front of any one diner unless requested. And of course, it should be picked up promptly.

At Chez Bob, waiters are paid less than minimum wage and they have to split their tips with the busboys, greeters and kitchen staff. Chez Bob is always understaffed and Chad was recently hired. His previous job was washing windows. He was thrown into the deep end and always feels a little out of his element. Today, his coworker, Annie, called in sick and he is covering her tables as well as his own. One of the custom-

ers in her section is a regular who orders food for an invisible friend and shouts at the waiter if he doesn't bring it and set it at perfect right angles. All of his customers are annoyed to begin with because Bob insists on overbooking. Many people call in reservations, don't show up, and never call to cancel. If everyone does show up, there is not enough room for them all. That means long waits for everyone and short tempers all around. Chad is keeping track of so many little things that they often get erased from his short-term memory before he has a chance to process them. Because he is overwhelmed, he is easily irritated by things—including you. Chad does not lack peripheral vision—he is ignoring you because he isn't ready to deal with your table just yet.

And the time when waiters seem most apt to get lost?—after they bring the check. Mentally, they have stopped worrying about you because your meal is done. It's easier to forget to pick up the check and bring change than it is to ignore someone waiving his arm shouting, "Waiter! I ordered soup an hour ago!"

221

WHAT DID I COME IN HERE FOR? OR DESTINESIA

See also what is the word?

It's like there's a force field between your bedroom and living room. You get up off the couch, propelled by a desire to get something. You pass through the door and poof!, your memory is gone. What am I doing in this room? I know I came in here for something.

You are not going insane, you just have insufficient RAM at this time. Your short term, or "working" memory, is analogous to the RAM on your computer. It is temporary storage of information you need to keep in your head while you perform tasks that require that information. There is a lot of information out there for the brain to process. You're not aware of much of the information your senses relay to the brain. While you are reading this, you are probably not thinking about your tongue. When your attention is brought to your tongue, however, you become aware of how it feels rubbing against that rough tooth in the back of your mouth.

That information was always there, but the brain was filtering it out. More than 99 percent of the sensory information that comes in is deemed irrelevant by the brain and it is not encoded into long-term memory. Some information needs to be in your consciousness just long enough to act on it—a decision to go into another room, for example.

"The first law of memory, in terms of cognitive processes is that in order to remember something—encode something in the brain—you have to pay attention to it," says Dr. Sonia Lupien, a neuropsychologist at Douglas Hospital in Montréal who specializes in the effects of stress on memory. "Many times when we 'forget' these little things, it's not even forgetting. It's not having encoded it in the first place."

Usually we do not concentrate on one task at a time. Our attention is divided. When you were sitting on the couch contemplating a trip into the bedroom, you were also thinking about what to make for dinner, whether the kids had done their homework, and how long it would be before your favorite show came on TV.

"Because we can not put everything into our memory, we decide what is relevant and should be encoded and what is not," Lupien says. "The more things you do at the same time, the less you are going to be able to say this one is relevant, this one is not. The probability that it doesn't even get in will explain why, when you get to the room you have no idea why you went there."

The reason older people seem to experience this more often is that many of the things their minds used to give priority to now fall into the less relevant category.

"If before it was important to know where your glasses were because you had four minutes to leave the house, you unconsciously would say 'here they are. I know they are here. This is important.' However, once you retire you have all the time in the world. Unconsciously it's not as important to find your glasses in .22 seconds. So you will not process this information in the same way."

Want to be sure to remember why you went into the room? Put it higher on your list of priorities.

WHAT IS THE WORD?

See also what did I come in here for?

I went to the store because I wanted... I had a recipe that called for.. You know, one of those green things... it's not a cantaloupe. It's a vegetable, you know... It's... uurrrggghhh. It's green...

Psychologists call this a "tip-of-the-tongue state." You know a word, you use it regularly, but your brain refuses to access it. Studies show that people between the ages of 18 and 22 experience this state about once or twice a week. Those between the ages of 65 and 75 lose words about twice as often.

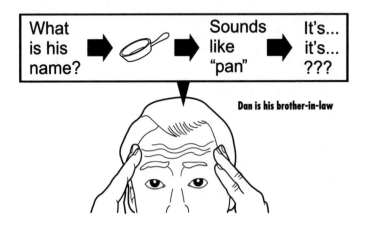

What is his name? ➡ 🍳 ➡ Sounds like "pan" ➡ It's... it's... ???

Dan is his brother-in-law

Sometimes a word pops into mind in a few seconds. Sometimes it takes days.

In the past, researchers speculated that the problem stemmed from a common word blocking a word that was similar to it. More recent studies suggest that people have the hardest time recalling a word like "duplicate" which is less common and sounds like few other words. Apparently the brain needs a bigger push to ferret out words we use less frequently.

Finding a word is actually a two-stage process. First the brain accesses the concept, and then it searches for the sound of the word to match the meaning. Something similar happens when you see a familiar face but you can't recall the person's name. Distinct nerve cell circuits serve the part of the brain that stores the visual information and another processes the word—the person's name.

Often people remember the first letter of the word or name, or a similar sounding word comes to mind. According to Deborah M. Burke, a psychology professor at Pomona College in Claremont, California, people are twice as likely to find the word if they read or hear something that shares some of the missing word's sounds.

A Dutch researcher, Willem Levelt of the Max Planck Institute for Psycholinguistics, used advanced brain-imaging technology to solve the problem. He likens tip-of-the-tongue to a traffic jam of the brain. He says the harder you try to find the word, the harder it becomes. Most people have had the experience of remembering the word an hour after the relevant conversation ended. It just "pops up." So far, the experts do not know why.

What they can tell you... Cucumber. That's the word I was looking for. Cucumber.

X-Y-Z

XMAS FOR CHRISTMAS THROUGH **ZIPPERS, STUCK**

XMAS FOR CHRISTMAS

Merry Xmas. It's meant as a holiday greeting, but to many, the "X" is a big irritant. Some dislike it because it's inelegant and not the way people speak. Others find it aggravating for religious reasons.

"Since someone mentioned that using 'Xmas' is taking the 'Christ' out of Christmas, I have never written 'Xmas,'" wrote a *Calgary Sun* reader. "Maybe a weird little hang-up, but working in reverse, every time I see the word 'Xmas' it's a little reminder to me that Christ belongs in Christmas!"

It may seem that Xmas is a symbol of our modern, secularized, commercialized, "I wanna Power Ranger" Christmas. Xmas, however, dates back to the 16th century. The X is a stand in for the Greek letter chi, which resembles our X. The name of Christ in Greek was Xristos, thus chi represented Christ. Its shape was also reminiscent of the cross. For these two reasons, Chi was used regularly in religious contexts. The Ninth-century *Book of Kells* contains a lavishly decorated chi-rho page. In the Sixteenth century, the use of Xmas spread

X=CHI

throughout Europe along with such words as "Xren" for "christen" and "Xtian" for "Christian." Christians of that time would, therefore, immediately recognize the "Christ" in "Xmas." We no longer do. Xmas is easier to fit into headlines and advertisements, however, which contributes to the modern perception that it is an attempt to secularize the holiday.

As for that other winter holiday spelling problem—Hanukkah, Hanuka, Chanukah... which is it? The answer is, it depends. Hanukkah is translated from Hebrew, which has a different alphabet. When linguists translate from a language that has a different set of characters, they try to approximate the sound with the letters of the second language as best they can. Hanukkah literally means "dedication." It refers to the rededication of the Temple in Jerusalem after it had been defiled by the Syrians. The first letter of the word is the Hebrew het, which is pronounced like the "ch" in the Scottish word loch. German, and thus the German-influenced Yiddish, pronounce the "ch" similarly, unlike in English where we would tend to see "ch" and pronounce it as in "chalk." Originally, the name of the holiday was transcribed Chanukkah. Because English speakers tended to pronounce Chanukkah incorrectly, the spelling evolved to begin with "H", which is a better English approximation. We still don't pronounce it quite right, but at least we get closer than when we try to pronounce it with a "Ch."

As for the middle of the word and the one k or two question— Hebrew has two letters that correspond to our K, *kaf* and *kof*. Hanukkah uses *kaf*, which has a stronger "k" sound. For that reason, it is often translated as a double K, but there aren't many words with two ks in English, thus, the double K doesn't convey much meaning to us and it is often dropped. As for the "h" at the end, it doesn't change the sound of "ah" and it is sometimes dropped. The most frequent variations you will see are Hanukkah or Chanukah.

YELLOW SPOTS ON PUBLIC TOILET SEATS, OR IF YOU SPRINKLE WHILE YOU TINKLE...

So you think men's restrooms are dirtier and grimier than women's? You're wrong. Dr. Charles Gerba, an Arizona microbiologist, has made a career of studying the places where germs lurk. As it turns out, women's facilities tend to have more harmful germs than men's. The researcher guesses this is because more children use them, putting the blame on young boys with bad aim.

There is another possibility. Women's restrooms have more bacteria because women use them. To avoid sitting on a dirty public toilet seat, many women squat or hover just above the bowl. It is not an easy task and they often miss the mark leaving drips and splashes on the seat.

The number of yellow drops has been increasing in stalls across America. It is a problem that builds upon itself. The more women hover and miss, the more spots they leave behind to remind us that the pots are not

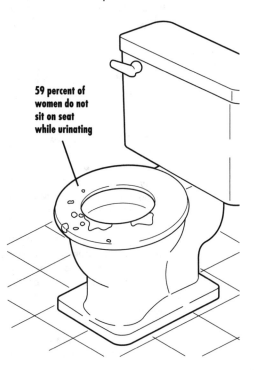

59 percent of women do not sit on seat while urinating

sanitary: The more women feel they are unsanitary, the more likely they are to hover. According to a recent study, about 59 percent of women now relieve themselves in this manner.

Let's dispel a few myths. You can't catch venereal disease from toilet seats. The American Social Health Association knows of no reported cases of transmission in this manner. To put it as delicately as possible, the parts of the anatomy that would carry sexually transmitted diseases do not actually come into contact with the toilet seat.

As Gerba told a *Salon* reporter, "You don't catch things off your butt. You catch things off your hands."

In a 1995 study, Gerba discovered that only one out of 59 public restroom toilet seats has E. Coli bacteria on it. He found much more bacteria on the sinks. Another study, three years later, revealed that the kitchen is much germier than the average bathroom. There are more than 200 times more fecal bacteria on a cutting board (from raw meat) than on the home toilet seat.

"If you have a choice between licking a toilet seat or a cutting board, go with the toilet seat," Gerba said.

The biggest danger from toilet seats is actually from injury, not disease. The Consumer Product Safety Commission reported that an estimated 44,335 people were treated in emergency rooms for toilet-related injuries in 1997, mostly from slipping and cracking various body parts on them.

A simple solution to the tinkle sprinkle problem is for women to do what men do. No, I don't mean standing to pee. Boys learn, early on, to lift the toilet seat to avoid hosing it. If women do not want to sit on the seat, there is no reason why they should not lift it as well.

Then again, maybe women *should* pee standing. Our urinating preferences are based as much on cultural conditioning as biology. A boy can easily sit down to urinate. A girl can, likewise, learn to pee standing although, admittedly, her aim is not as good as her brother's. That is the contention of Denise Decker, a nurse from California who maintains a Web page devoted to teaching women the skill. If you'd like to know more about it, the URL is www.restrooms.org/standing.html.

"YOUR CALL IS IMPORTANT TO US": ON HOLD

See also caught in traffic, lines, waiters, really bad

My call is not important to you! If my call were so important to you, you'd answer it!

An item from the "I could have told you that for free" file: A study conducted for Prudential Insurance of America found that 41 percent of Americans surveyed grew "angrier and an-

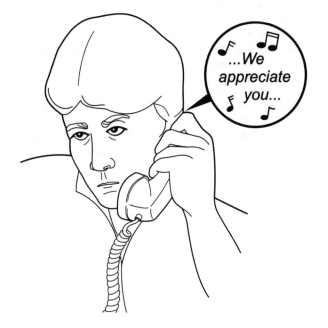

...We appreciate you...

grier by the minute" when put on hold.

Yes, but why? Anthropologist David Murray says it's cultural. Westerners, especially Americans, are action focused. We only feel alive during an event. The rest of the time doesn't count. "We feel as if we're hibernating," Murray told the *Washington Post*. "Waiting is an insult to us. We feel we're being put down when forced to wait. We have a sense we've been disrespected; hence, the anger."

Robert Levine, the psychologist who wrote *A Geography of Time*, chalks it up to a power struggle. People with power and money can make others wait. Therefore, if you're being made to wait, your social status is being demeaned.

"There is no greater symbol of domination," he says, "since time is the only possession which can in no sense be replaced."

Expect to be angered a great deal in the future. Being stuck on hold is not something that's going to vanish. A recent article in *Marketing Tools* reveals that instead of trying to reduce hold times, businesses are trying to find ways to entertain you while you wait. A number of companies are springing up to provide "messages on hold." Most of their clients use the service to bombard you with marketing messages. We hate this—so why do they do it? Because we lie. Despite what we say, messages on hold keep us on the line. A Nationwide Insurance study shows that on-hold messaging reduces hang-ups by 50–80 percent. In fact, 15–35 percent of callers responded to the advertising messages and bought additional items.

Thank you for continuing to hold. Your call is important to us. Please hold for a message from our sponsor...

ZIPPERS, STUCK

The metal-toothed clothing fastener dates back to 1891 and a Chicago inventor named Whitcomb Judson. It wasn't until 1917 that a Swedish engineer named Gideon Sunback updated the design so it resembled the fastener we know today. The word "zipper" began life as a trade name. The B.F. Goodrich company marketed a model of galoshes with a hookless fastener. The brand name of the shoes was soon applied to their new-fangled fastener. As zippers gained popularity, more

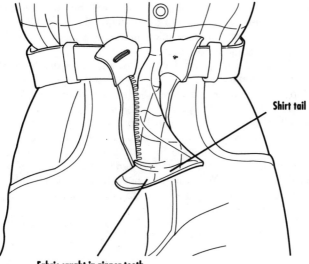

Shirt tail

Fabric caught in zipper teeth

and more people were able to experience the joys of having a zip stick at an inopportune moment.

If you take a close look at a zipper—to avoid misunderstandings you should probably make it your own—you will see that it is made up of a slider with a pull that runs over two rows of molded metal or plastic teeth which are shaped in such a way that they interlock. Most often it is the slider that breaks down. If you find your zipper just won't zip, or if it has the unfortunate habit of leaving you exposed to the public, the slider is probably worn or bent out of shape. Ditto if it seems welded in place. A common way for sliders to become bent is fabric that gets caught in the zip's teeth. Pull the thread out of the zip. If you still can't get the thing open, you can try greasing the zipper with crayons, candles, soap or lip balm. Once you get the offending item off, you can fix the slider by gently squeezing it back into shape with a pair of pliers. "Gently" is the active word here. You want to squeeze it just enough to keep it from sliding down the teeth or open it just enough to move freely, not enough to seal it shut or break it in half. If the zipper is missing teeth or it is coming off the fabric all together, this is more complicated. If you can sew, you can fix it. If you can't, call a tailor.

While we're on the subject of stuck zippers, briefly, here's what *Men's Health* has to say about getting stuck in your zipper. While it is extremely rare that anyone gets his entire member stuck like the boy in the movie *There's Something About Mary*, minor mishaps do happen. Zipper accidents usually result in superficial skin injuries but they are still painful enough to make #3 on the magazine's list of the "8 Worst Things You Can Do to Your Privates." Contrary to popular belief, most zipper injuries occur when unzipping, not zipping. If you find yourself in this position, *Men's Health* advises you pull the zipper in the direction it came from in one swift motion. Then assess the damage and, if necessary, apply a bandage to stop the bleeding.

BIBLIOGRAPHY

Abraham, Spencer. "The Case for Needed Legal Reform." *USA Today*, July 1, 1998.

Abrahams, Marc, ed. *Best of Annals of Improbable Research.* New York: W. H. Freeman and Company, 1998.

Achenbach, Joel. *Why Things Are.* New York: Ballantine Books, 1991.

Adams, Cecil. "Everything You Ever Wanted to Know About Farts." *The Straight Dope,* Chicago Reader, Inc, 1996.

———. "Why is the Sound of Fingernails Scraping a Blackboard so Annoying?" *The Straight Dope [syndicated column],* Chicago Reader Inc. 1996.

Ajluni, Cheryl. "Static elimination technology rids computer screens and television sets of static electric fields." *Electronic Design,* November 18, 1996.

Aisling, Irwin. "Scientists Get the Art of Dunking Down to a T." *Daily Telegraph,* November 25, 1998.

Allison, Wes. "The Worst Job Ever? Paid Patients Unzip to Aid Med Students." *The Washington Times,* January 15, 2001.

Allmon, Stephanie. "The Privy Truth: Toilet Seats Getting A Bad Rap." *Palm Beach Post,* May 16, 2000.

———. "Are Airlines Missing the Flight?" *Prepared Foods,* June 1998.

Armour, Stephanie. "Rage Against the Machine. Technology's Burps Give Workers Heartburn." *USA Today,* August 16, 1999.

Asbell, Bernard and Karen Wynn. *What They Know About You.* New York: Random House, 1991.

———. Associated Press. "Why won't that machine take my dollar?" *Arlington Morning News,* May 30, 1999.

Barbash, Fred. "Terminal Tantrums." *The Washington Post,* June 7, 1999.

Baum, Stephanie L. "Cities, Schools Take Aim at Laser Pointers." *Christian Science Monitor,* December 24, 1998.

Bennett, Andrea. "Stranded at an airport recently? Cut your wait with our flight delay survival guide." *Money,* January 1, 2001.

Bensman, Todd. "Pair Arrested in Luggage Thefts." *Dallas Morning News,* April 24, 1998.

Bendman, Hillary. "Web Site Sells Unclaimed Baggage." *University Wire,* March 16, 2001.

Blair, James W. "Cost-Cutting Cops Seek to Avoid False Alarms." *Christian Science Monitor,* February 24, 1998.

Bliatto, Tom. "Controversy: Fossil Fool Barney and Friends..." *People,* June 21, 1993.

Bloomfield, Louis. "How Things Work,"

Bowen, Jon. "Personal-space Invaders." *Salon,* September 1, 1999.

Bowles, Scott. "Aggressive ticketing has drivers feeling trapped." *USA Today,* September 3, 1999.

Brock, Barbara J. "TV Free Families: Are They Lola Granolas, Normal Joes or High and Holy Snots." Http://www.tvturnoff.org/BrockRsearchSummary.htm.

Brodeur, Raymond, D.C., PhD. "The Audible Release Associated with Joint Manipulation." *Journal of Manipulative and Physiological Therapeutics.* March/April 1995.

Brody, Jane. "Slaying a Case of Dragon Mouth." *Minneapolis Star Tribune,* March 23, 1997.

Brody, Leslie. "Laser Pointers Termed a Danger." *The Record (Bergen County, NJ),* October 7, 1998.

Brown, Jeanette. "#$@%&! THIS MACHINE." *Business Week,* March 22, 1999.

Brumley, Al. "Radio Innovator Has A New Blueprint for FM." *Dallas Morning News,* July 14, 1996.

———. "Solid Old: Radio Dials for Dollars by Programming More and More of the Past." *Dallas Morning News,* November 14, 1998.

Bryant, Adam et al. "Why Flying Is So Awful" *Newsweek,* July 10, 2000.

Bryant, Furlow. "The Smell of Love: How Women Rate the Sexiness and pleasantness of a Man's Body.." *Psychology Today,* March 13, 1996.

Burgess, John. "Even Translated, Error Messages May Mean Kaboom!" *Washington Post,* October 14, 1998.

Burkeman, Oliver. "Keep Your Distance." *The Guardian [UK],* September 14, 1999.

Butler, David. "Best Alarm is Not False." *Minneapolis Star Tribune,* March 21, 1996

Butler, Jerry. "Mosquitoes Have Discriminating Tastes, UF Researchers Find." Press Release. August 20, 1999.

Cadre, Adam. "And a Purple Dinosaur Shall Lead Them: Barney and the Future of Intergenerational Politics." *Bad Subjects,* Issue #12, March, 1994.

Carlson, Peter. "Playing the Waiting Game; Stuck in Line at the ATM? Still On Hold for the Doctor? Got Something Better to Do With Your Time? Here, Read This." *The Washington Post,* December 14, 1999.

Carpenter, Dave. "Rude Ringers. Complaints Rise with Cell Phone Use." *Washington Times,* August 2, 2000.

———. "Carry On Meals And Fly." *Food Institute Report,* January 26, 1999.

Castellanos, Jorge & David Azelrod, "Effect of Habitual Knuckle Cracking on Hand Function." *Annals of Rheumatic Diseases,* Vol. 49, 1990.

Catlett, Jason. "What Can Be Done About Junk E-Mail?" *USA Today Magazine,* November 1, 1998.

Chebat, Jean-Charles-Gelinas et al. "The Impact of Mood on Time Perceptions, Memorization and Acceptance of Waiting." *Genetic, Social & General Psychology Monographs,* November 1, 1995.

———. "Chewing on Tinfoil Can Kill Germs." *Wireless Flash News Service,* February 27, 1998.

Christensen, Damaris. "Is Snoring a DiZZZZease?" *Science News,* March 11, 2000.

Chism, Olin. "Show must go on, but coughs must go off." *The Dallas Morning News,* August 25, 1996.

Christman, Laura. "In Your Dust: We're Talking About The Common Household Variety - It's a Veritable Breakdown of Your Life." *Newsday,* March 26, 1998.

Connor, Steve. "Biscuit Dunking Perfected." *Independent,* November 25, 1998.

Corey, Mary. "Raising a Stink Over Scent." *The Evening Post (Wellington, New Zealand),* September 20, 1995.

Coventry, John. "Periodontal disease. (ABC of Oral Health)" *British Medical Journal*, July 1, 2000.

Cribb, Robert. "Etiquette for a wired world." *The Toronto Star*, December 6, 1998.

Debarros, Anthony. "Radio's Historic Change Amid Consolidation." *USA Today*, July 7, 1998.

Decker, Denise. "A Woman's Guide to How to Pee Standing Up." www.restrooms.org/standing.html.

Desrocher, Jack. "Oral ecology." *Technology Review*, January 1, 1997.

Diaz, Kevin. "Getting a Handle on Stray-cart Blues." *Minneapolis Star Tribune*, April 5, 1999.

Digital Learning Center for Microbial Ecology. "Habitat On Humanity." Michigan State University Communication Technology Laboratory Center for Microbial Ecology, 2000.

DiPacio, Bonnie. "Why are Clowns So Scary to Some? Figures of Fantasy both Attract, Repel." *Dallas Morning News*, January 17, 1999.

Drake, Petra. E-mail correspondence with author. April, 2001.

Dufner, Edward. "Experts Call Virus Writers High-Tech, Low-Brow." *Dallas Morning News*, April 1, 1999.

Durant, Zachary. Telephone Interview by Author. March 13, 2001.

Eagan, James M. *A Speeder's Guide to Avoiding Tickets.* New York: Avon Books, 1990.

Ebeling, Walter. "Urban Entomology." University of California, Division of Agricultural Sciences, 1996.

———. "Echo Cancellation," *Computer Desktop Encyclopedia*, January 1, 1998.

Edwards, Bob. "First Class vs. Coach." Morning Edition (NPR), May 26, 1998.

Ehrlich, Robert. *Why Toast Lands Jelly-Side Down.* Princeton, New Jersey: Princeton University Press, 1997.

Evans, Sandra. "Send In the Clowns, But Not Too Close." *Washington Post*, March 28, 2000.

Everbach, Tracy. "Huh? Academic Jargon is the Language of a Closed Club Among Scholars." *Dallas Morning News*, July 6, 1999.

Finberg, Kathy. "Telemarketing Calls are Not Good RX." *The Arizona Republic*, March 9, 1999.

Fisher, Anne. "Best Business Books: Excuse Me, Please, Do You Mind If I Sell You Something?" *Fortune*, June 21, 1999.

Fishman, Charles. "But Wait, You Promised..." *Fast Company*, April 1, 2001.

Flaim, Denise. "The Science of Stockings. We Can Orbit a Space Shuttle, Splice a Gene, Smash and Atom. Why Can't We Create Pantyhose That Don't Run?" *Newsday*, November 18, 1993.

Flatow, Ira. "Analysis: How the Sense of Smell Operates." Talk of the Nation Science Friday (NPR), March 10, 2000.

———. "Analysis: Types and habits of some of the many insects that reappear as spring comes." Talk of the Nation Science Friday (NPR), March 24, 2001.

———. *Rainbows, Curve Balls and Other Wonders of the Natural World Explained.* New York: Harper and Row, 1988.

Forsman, Theresa. "To Zagat Reviewers, Good Service Sells." *The Record* (Bergen County, NJ), September 2, 1999.

Frase-Blunt, Martha. "The Cubicles Have Ears. Maybe They Need Earplugs; A Psychologist Says Noisy Pod Farms Make for Jumpy Workers." *The Washington Post*, March 6, 2001.

Fumento, Michael. "Senseless Scent Patrol." *The Washington Times*, May 7, 2000.

Getchell, Annie. "Zipper Mending: How to Make Quick-Fixes and Permanent Repairs." *Backpacker*, August 1, 1996.

Gillespie, Nick. "Time and a Half." *Reason*, May 1, 1998.

Glanz, James. "No Hope of Silencing the Phantom Crinklers of the Opera." *New York Times*, June 1, 2000.

Glausiusz, Josie. "The Root of All Itching." *Discover*, April 2001.

Goddard, Peter. "The science behind the scent." *The Toronto Star*, January 11, 2001.

Goldman, Michael. "Clowns are No Laughing Matter." *Toronto Star*, July 8, 2000.

Goodman, Tim. "Good Commercials are Eating Up More Time." *Minneapolis Star Tribune*, June 2, 1998.

Gorman, Christine. "Shake, Rattle and Roar. Thunder in the Distance? No, It's a Boom Car Coming." *Time*, March 6, 1989.

Gott, Peter. "Tomato Juice and the Piles." *The Ottawa Sun*, June 17, 2000.

Graedon, Joe and Theresa Graedon. "The People's Pharmacy: How to be Unattractive- to the Mosquitoes." *Newsday*, August 14, 2000.

Grabmeier, Jeff. "Credit Card Debt May Be Bad For Your Health." *Newswire*, March 1, 2000.

Grant, Elaine X. "Tasteful Choices (Airline Food Service)" *Travel Agent*, August 23, 1999.

Griest, Stephanie. "Telemarketers often get wrung out by the stress in their work." *Minneapolis Star Tribune*, July 14, 1995.

Groves, Bob. "Calming the ZZZZZZs." *The Record* (Bergen County, NY), January 18, 1993.

Gubbins, Teresa. "What About MY Space?" *Dallas Morning News*, February 23, 2000.

Guernsey, Lisa. "Taking the Offensive Against Cell Phones." *New York Times*, January 11, 2001.

Haege, Glenn. "Stop Mosquitoes from Bugging You with Several Simple Solutions." *Gannett News Service*, August 22, 2000.

Hai, Dorothy M. "Sex and the Single Armrest: Use of Personal Space During Air Travel." *Psychological Reports*, v. 51, 1982.

Hainer, Cathy. "How the Music Industry Got Out of Tune with Its Artists." USA Today, April 10, 1996.

Hall, Gerry. "Tracking the Path of Lost Baggage." *Toronto Star*, January 16, 1999.

Hample, Scott. "Endangered Species." *Marketing Tools*, May 1995.

Hamer, Dean and Peter Copeland. *Living With Our Genes.* New York: Doubleday, 1998.

"Hangnails." *Dermatology Times*, July 2000.

Hansen, Diane and Jesse Sheidlower. "Seasonal Words." *Weekend Sunday* (NPR), December 27, 1998.

Hansen, Laura. "Dialing for Dollars." *Marketing Tools*, January/February 1997.

Hanson, Eric. "A Tragedy of manners. A Funny Thing Happened on the Way to Decorum." *Minneapolis Star Tribune*, April 7, 2000.

Harley, Trevor A and Helen E. Brown. "What Causes a Tip-of-the-Tongue State? Evidence for Lexical Neighbour-hood Effects in Speech Production." *British Journal of Psychology*. February 1, 1998.

Haubrich, William S. *Medical Meanings, A Glossary of Word Origins*. Philadelphia: American College of Physicians, 1997.

Hawkins, Katherine. Telephone interview by author, March 13, 2001.

Hayden, Thomas. "The Scent of Human." *U.S. News & World Report*, March 26, 2001.

Helm, Ted. "An Overview of Nonverbal Communication in Impersonal Relationships."

Hellmich, Nanci. "Sharing Tips for Both Waiters and Diners." *USA Today*, June 22, 1994.

Hendricks, Gary. "Newer Systems Keep Passengers, Bags Together." *Atlanta Constitution*, February 21, 2000.

Henrich, Greve, R. "Patterns of Competition: The Diffusion of a Market Position in Radio Broadcasting." *Administrative Science Quarterly*, March 1, 1996.

Heymann, Thomas N. *On An Average Day*. New York: Ballantine Books, 1989.

Hetts, Suzanne and Daniel Estep. "Tree Scratches Actually Signals." *Denver Rocky Mountain News*, June 24, 2000.

———. "How to Fix a Jumpy CD." *Minneapolis Star Tribune*, March 25, 2000.

Hoyt, Carolyn. "Development: How Memory Develops From the moment of birth." *Parenting*, October 1, 1999.

Hulihan, J. "Ice Cream Headache." *British Medical Journal*, May 10, 1997.

Huston, Aletha C. et al. *Big World, Small Screen: The Role of Television in American Society*. Lincoln, Nebraska: University of Nebraska Press, 1992.

Huntington, Sharon. "On the Trail of Dust." *The Christian Science Monitor*, August 17, 1999.

Hutchins, Chris. "Brain Freeze! Is There No Escape From That Icy Ache?" *Arlington Morning News*, July 18, 1999.

Hyde, Justin. "Detroit to Push Cars that Warn of Traffic Jams." *The Toronto Star*, Oct 23, 2000.

———. "Ice Cream Headaches, Nerves Tied." *Arizona Republic*, February 15, 2000.

———. "If the Movie Trailer's Rockin' Don't Bother Knockin' It." *Toronto Star*, January 20, 1999.

Incantalupo, Tom. "Alarming. Even Turning Your Car Into an Electronic Fortress May Not Keep it Safe." *St. Louis Post-Dispatch*, October, 30, 1993.

Ingram, Jay. "Why Candy Wrappers Can Wreck Your Night Out." *Toronto Star*, July 16, 2000.

Irvine, Pru. "@/+!=′!****!!! Road Rage Has Got Nothing on This." *Independent*, December 11, 1997.

"It's Enough to Make You Sick [Word Origins]." *Medical Post*, November 17, 1999.

Ivry, Bob. "Why You Mind Very Much if They Do." *The Record (Bergen County, NJ)*, July 16, 2000.

Jacobs, Jerry A. "Measuring Time at Work: Are Self-Reports Accurate?" *Monthly Labor Review*, December 1, 1998.

Jacobson, Louis. "Sensor-Based Cruise Control Keeps Cars Apart." *The Washington Post*, September 4, 2000.

James, Leon and Diane Nahl. Telephone interview by author. January 24, 2001.

———. *Road Rage and Aggressive Driving: Steering Clear of Highway Warfare*. Amherst, NY: Prometheus Books, 2000.

Jaret, Peter. "What Pests Want in Your Home." *National Wildlife*, August 1, 1999.

Jenkins, Milly. "A Virus is Not Always the Product of a Sick Mind." *Independent*, January 13, 1998.

Johnson, Kirk A "Age-Old Questions and All the Answers You Need to Live A Healthier Life." *Health Quest: The Publication of Black Wellness*, October 31, 1995.

Kadir, Rahimah A. "Plaque - The Hidden Enemy." *New Straits Times*, February 1, 1998.

Kane, Joseph Nathan. *Famous First Facts*. New York: The H.W. Wilson Company, 1954.

Kang, Y. Peter. "I Warned You!" *University Wire*, November 8, 1999.

Kanner, Bernice. *Are You Normal?* New York: St. Martin's, 1995.

Karger, Dave. "Trailer Trash: Are Movie Previews Giving Away Too Much These Days?" *Entertainment Weekly*, July 10, 1998.

Kassirer, Jerome and Marcia Angell. "Losing Weight- An Ill-Fated New Year's Resolution." *New England Journal of Medicine*, January 1, 1998.

Kato, Hidetoshi. "Crowd as the Social Environment." 1972. http://www.chubu.ac.jp/inst/professors/webdoc8.htm

Kelleher, Kathleen. "The Word is... I know, It's Right on the Tip of my Tongue." *Minneapolis Star Tribune*, April 9, 1997.

Kelly, Sara, "When Bad Breath Happens to Good People." *Men's Health*, October 1, 1996.

Kington, Miles. "Just a Mot, The Professor is Giving Advice." *Independent*, June 2, 1997.

Kinnaird, Kevin. "Focus on cranking out loud sound." *The Washington Times*, June 11, 1999.

Klein, Richard. "Get a Whiff of This: Breaking the Smell Barrier." *New Republic*, February 6, 1995.

Kline, Hanne K. "Press 1 to Streamline." *The Dallas Morning News*, July 26, 1997.

Koepp, Stephen. "Gridlock: Congestion on Americas Highways and Runways Takes a Grinding Toll." *Time*, September 12, 1998.

Krugman, Dean M, Cameron, Glen T, and White, Candace McKearney, "Visual Attention to Programming and Commercials." *Journal of Advertising*, March 1, 1995.

Kurtzweil, Paula. "Dental More Gentle with Painless 'Drillings' and Matching Fillings." *FDA Consumer*, May 1, 1999.

238

Lafavore, Michael. "The Best, the Worst and the Really Weird: Our 4th Annual Collection of Advice, Warnings, News, Folly and Opinion." *Men's Health*, January 1, 1994.

Larson, Jan. "Surviving Commuting." *American Demographics*, July, 1998.

Lehndorff, John. "A Tip to the Wise. Poor Service Has Driven Some Diners to Get Tough." *Denver Rocky Mountain News*, October 19, 2000.

Lipscomb, Betsy. Telephone Interview by Author. April 4, 2001.

Lloyd, Nancy. "What You Don't Know About Credit Can Cost You." *Minneapolis Star Tribune*, May 23, 1996.

Long, Karen Haymon. "Woes of Those on the Go." *Tampa Tribune*, June 25, 2000.

Lupien, Sonia. Telephone Interview by Author. March 22, 2001.

Malone, Barbara. "Holding Onto the Wheel." *The World & I*, February 1, 1996.

Maney, Kevin. "PowerPoint Obsession Takes Off." *USA Today*, May 12, 1999.

Margo, Jill. "Tail Wind." *Sydney Morning Herald*, February 2, 1995.

Marriott, Michel. "Some New CD Players Really Don't Skip." *Minneapolis Star Tribune*, March 24, 2000.

Masoff, Joy. *Oh Yuck! The Encyclopedia of Everything Nasty.* New York: Workman Publishing, 2000.

Matthews, Robert. "Odd Socks: A Cominatoric Example of Murphy's Law." *Mathematics Today*, March-April 1996.

——. "Tumbling Toast, Murphy's Law and the Fundamental Constants." *European Journal of Physics*, 16 172-173, 1995.

——. "Strange But True: Why We'd All Be Safer Taking a Few More Risks." *The Sunday Telegraph*, August 16, 1998.

——. "Why Some Words Just Will Not Trip Off the Tongue." *The Sunday Telegraph*. May 31, 1998.

Mayer, Caroline. "Today's Specials: Waiters with Professional Training." *St. Louis Post-Dispatch*, April 13, 1993.

McAndrew, Francis T. Telephone interview by author, March 28, 2001.

McCluggage, Denise. "For Safe Driving, Have a Clear Outlook." *Washington Times*, July 2, 1999.

McCombs, Phil. "Something to Chew On." *Washington Post*, November 7, 2000.

McKay, Martha. "Nuisance Calls Hit New Highs." *The Record (Bergen County, NJ)*, January 30, 2000.

McMurran, Kristin and Donald A. Norman. "So You're Still Having Trouble Making Those Christmas Toys Work? Don't Worry. It's Not Your Fault." People, January 9, 1989.

McNamee, Laurence McNamee and Kent Biffle. "Funny Bone?" *The Dallas Morning News*, January 12, 1997.

Melody, William H. "Satellite Communications." *The 1998 Canadian Encyclopedia*, September 6, 1997.

Mercuri, Rebecca, PhD. E-mail correspondence with author. January 21, 2001.

Miller, Norman. "The Worm Has Returned." *Independent on Sunday*, November 3, 1996.

Mindess, Mary. Telephone interview by author. February 21, 2001.

Mizejewski, Gerald. "Man gets breathing room after 10 years of hiccups." *The Washington Times*, March 25, 2000.

Montague, Claudia. "Hold Everything." *Marketing Tools*, May 1995.

Most, Doug. "Driving 65 MPH is Good for Egos, But Little Else." *The Record (Bergen County, NJ)*, February 2, 1998.

Munson, Marty. "Head off itches. (controlling the urge to scratch)" *Prevention*, May 1, 1996.

——. "Murkowski Praises UAL Decision to Add Space Between Airline Seats." *Capitol Hill Press Releases*, August 6, 1999.

Murphy, William. "It's Simply Alarming: Bill Would Ban Noisy Anti-Theft Devices on Cars." *Newsday*, April 28, 1997.

Muse, Melinda. *I'm Afraid, You're Afraid.* New York: Hyperion, 2000.

——. "My Doctor Said I Don't Need Surgery for my Hemorrhoids!" *Medical Update*, August 1, 1994.

Myers, D.G. "Bad Writing." *Weekly Standard*, May 10, 1999.

Myslinski, Norbert R. "Now Where Did I Put Those Keys?" *The World & I*, November 1, 1998.

Nayder, Jim. Telephone interview by author. February 6, 2001.

Neff, Raymond K. "Teleworld." *The World & I*, May 1, 2000.

Newell, Anne L. "Carts Come in a Variety of Colors and Sizes." *Arizona Republic*, July 3, 1999.

Ng, Bernice. "British researchers say cell phones may play role in attraction." *University Wire*, February 15, 2001.

——. "No More Flunking on Dunking." *BBC News Online Network*, November 25, 1999.

Norman, Donald. *The Design of Everyday Things.* New York: Doubleday, 1988.

Norvig, Peter, "The Making of the Gettysburg PowerPoint Presentation." www.norvig.com/Gettysburg/making.html

Numez, Daniel G. "Cause and Effects of Noise Pollution." Student Paper Interdisciplinary Minor in Global Sustainability, University of California, Irvine. Spring 1998. http://www.cnlm.uci.edu/~sustain/global/sensem/S98/Nunez/Noise.html

Okie, Susan. "Survivors; 350 Million Years Later, Cockroaches Are Still Going Strong." *The Washington Post*, November 10, 1999.

Okorafor, Nnedi. "Remember– Computers are Human Too." *University Wire*, July 6, 1998.

Perl, Peter. "Waking With the Enemy; He Never Quite Believed he Had a Snoring Problem Till He Slept Beside a Tape Recorder." *The Washington Post*, November 28, 1999.

Perry, Avi. "Echo Cancellers." *Wireless Review,* February 1, 2000.

Pirroni, Marco. Telephone interview by author, March 15, 2001.

Precker, Michael. "Germ Warfare From a Man Who's 'Written a Lot of Toilet Papers,'" *Dallas Morning News,* July 20, 1998.

———. "Productivity per Square Foot." *Nation's Restaurant News,* November 6, 2000.

Quinn, Jane Bryant Quinn. "Beware of Bank Card Fees." *St. Louis Post-Dispatch,* August 20, 1996.

Ragsdale, Shirley. "Passenger Trust Must be Rebuilt by Service, Smiles." *Gannett News Service,* July 13, 2000.

Raphael, Michael. "This Space is Mine! Drivers Show Classic Apelike Behavior." Associated Press, May 13, 1997.

Rayner, Ben. "Boom!" *The Toronto Star,* September 23, 1998.

Reynolds, Christopher. "Odds of Major U.S. Airlines Losing Your Baggage Are About One in 197." *Minneapolis Star Tribune,* July 16, 2000.

Rheingold, Howard. *They Have a Word For It.* Los Angeles: Jeremy P. Tarcher, Inc. 1988.

Riechmann, Deb. "TV Commercials Giving Viewers an Earful." *AP Online,* May 28, 1998.

Rivenburg, Roy. "Sound of Silence: It's Disquieting Are We Addicted to Noise?" *St. Louis Post-Dispatch,* July 28, 1997.

Roach, Mary. "Ladies Who Spray." *Salon,* May 19, 2000.

Robinson, John P. and Geoffrey Godbey. "The great American Slowdown." *American Demographics,* June 1, 1996.

———. *Time for Life: The Surprising Ways Americans Use Their Time.* University Park, Pennsylvania: Pennsylvania State University Press, 1997.

Robinson, William. "What's the Top Pest?: Ants are the Answer." *Pest Control,* April 1, 1999.

Roman, Mar. "I Sing the Body Electric (Causes Behind Peculiar Health Symptoms)." *Men's Health,* June 1, 1996.

Rose, Heidi. "Human Weakness Causes Virus Spread." *Computer Weekly,* August 3, 2000.

Sant, Charles. E-mail correspondence with author. November, 1997.

Sapsted, David. "Loud Music is As Addictive as Drugs and Alcohol." *Daily Telegraph,* December 10, 1998.

Schwade, Steve. "Read This Before You Fly: Prevention's Flight Plan for Comfort and Health." Prevention, June 1, 1996.

Schwarcz, Joe. "Everyday Chemistry: What Makes a Situation Sticky." *Washington Post,* December 8, 1999.

"Scientists Look for Commonalities in Annoying Sounds." All Things Considered [NPR], May 12, 1998.

Scott, John. "Road Rage." Fox Files (Fox News Network), June 22, 1999.

Segal, David. "They Sell Songs the Whole World Sings: Mass Merchants Offer Convenience, Less Choice." *The Washington Post,* February 21, 2001.

Saketkhoo K, Januszkievicz A, Sackner MA. "Effects of drinking hot water, cold water, and chicken soup on nasal mucus velocity and nasal airflow resistance." *Chest* 1978;74(4):408-10.

Schwartz, John. "No Love for Computer Bugs: A New Generation of Virus Hunters Learn the Craft." *The Washington Post,* July 5, 2000.

Shuler, Lou. "Your Body Problems Solved." *Men's Health,* April 1, 1999.

Sidener, Jonathan. "Happy Birthday, Cubicle." *The Arizona Republic,* October 3, 1998.

Siegel, Robert. "Interview: Professor Eric Kramer, Simon's Rock College, Discusses the Scientific Reason Why Plastic Candy Wrappers Make Noise When You Unwrap Them." All Things Considered (NPR), June 1, 2000.

Siegfried, Tom. "Making Memories: Science Provides Scattered Picture of Remembering." *Dallas Morning News,* April 20, 1998.

Simon, Scott. "Brain Freeze." Weekend Saturday (NPR), July 12, 1997.

Sleigh, J.W. "Ice Cream Headache." *British Medical Journal,* September 6, 1997.

"Snooze Alarm: Snoring and Your Health." *Discover,* July 1, 1999.

Snyder, Jodie. "It may seem funny, but no one knows why we hic." *Minneapolis Star Tribune,* July 2, 1995.

Smith, Dinitia. "When Ideas Get Lost in Bad Writing." *New York Times,* February 27, 1999.

Smith, Ian K. "Personal Time: Your Health: Dangerous Seats? Crammed into Airline Economy Class You May Be Risking Blood Clots." *Time,* November 6, 2000.

Snead, Elizabeth. "Sneak Peeks. First Impressions Are the Most Important. Just Ask Anyone Who Saw the Trailer for The Postman." *USA Today,* May 1, 1998.

Spake, Amanda and Dana Hawkins, Katy Kelly, Leonard Wiener. "Relief for Famished Fliers." *U.S. News and World Report,* May 8, 2000.

Spilner, Maggie. "De-stress Your Commute." *Prevention,* March 1, 1995.

Steinbach, Alice. "Buyers Dig Up Many Treasures at Graveyard of Lost Airline Bags." *Minneapolis Star Tribune,* August 25, 1996.

Stern, Jane and Michael. *The Encyclopedia of Bad Taste.* New York: HarperCollins, 1990.

Stewart, Martha. "Hankies And Dust: Nothing To Sneeze At." *Newsday,* April 12, 2000.

Stewart, Thomas A. "Ban it Now! Friends Don't Let Friends Use PowerPoint." *Fortune.com,* February 5, 2001.

"Stickiness: Blame it on the Bubbles." *The Economist,* January 23, 1999.

Stovsky, Renee. "No! No! Not Again. What Happens When Kids Love to Hear Books Their Parents Hate to Read?" *St. Louis Post-Dispatch,* September 5, 1993.

Stuard, Doug. "Voice Quality in PCS and Cellular Networks: Eliminating the Echo." *Lighting Dimensions,* September 1, 1998.

240

Sugarman, Carole. "Use it or Lose It; Do You Know When It's Time to Chuck the Chicken or Dump the Milk?" *The Washington Post,* October 11, 2000.

Suplee, Curt. "Get Outta My Space! The Science and Secrets of Personal Space." *The Washington Post,* June 9, 1999.

Sykes, Charles J. *A Nation of Victims.* New York: St. Martin's Press, 1992.

————. "Take My Dandruff....Please." *Newsday,* December 12, 1994

Tilley, Steve. "Please Carefully Read the Following Warning Before Proceeding." *Edmonton Sun,* January 27, 2000.

Tenner, Edward. *When Things Bite Back: Technology and the Revenge of Unintended Consequences.* New York: Alfred A. Knopf, 1996.

Terrell, Kenneth and Sara Hammel. "Call of the Riled." *U.S. News & World Report,* June 14, 1999.

Tevlin, Jon. "Dial 'R' for Rage. So You Expected to Talk to Someone? No, No, No." *Minneapolis Star Tribune,* November 15, 1999.

————. "Tricks of the Trailers: Draw 'Em In, But Spoil the Movie." *Minneapolis Star Tribune,* October 26, 1999.

Uhlig, Robert. "Bad Breath Detector Has the Measure of Halitosis." *Daily Telegraph,* October 21, 1999.

————. "UK Restricts Use of Laser Light Pens." *Medical Post,* December 2, 1997.

————. "Understanding Colds." www.commoncold.org.

Underwood, Anne and Pat Wingert et al. "Stress in the Skies." *Newsweek,* November 29, 1999.

————. "University Tries to Bring Some Class to Airline Foodservice." *Nation's Restaurant News,* October 16, 2000.

————. "Update: A survey of recent findings published in academic journals." *Independent,* July 2, 1997

————. "Update on ... chewing-gum." *Independent,* February 11, 1997.

Van Der Werf, Martin. "Adverse Reaction. Product Plugs Lose Punch Amid Commercial Overload." *Arizona Republic,* July 26, 1998.

Veilleux, Zachary, "The 8 Worst Things You Can Do to Your Privates." *Men's Health,* November 1, 1998

Viets, Elaine. "Hosiery History: From Silk to Pantyhose." *St. Louis Post-Dispatch,* May 6, 1993.

————. "Virus Attacks Cost Organizations $17.1 Billion in 2000." *Computer Economics Press Release,* January 5, 2001.

Von Radowitz, John. "Motoring: Why road rage and murder are too close for comfort." *Birmingham Post,* January 5, 2001.

Wallace, Patricia M. *The Psychology of the Internet.* Cambridge, United Kingdom: Cambridge University Press, 1999.

Wann, Marilyn. *Fat! So?* Berkley, California: Ten Speed Press, 1998.

Ward, Robert. "Loud Music Stimulates Sex Center in the Brain." *Daily Telegraph,* February 17, 2000.

————. "We All Scream After Ice Cream." *Independent,* May 10, 1997.

————. "Wellness and Self-Responsibility." *Ardell Wellness Report,* January 20, 1998.

Werts, Diane. "Glued to the Tube. Time for Entertaining Reality." *Newsday,* April 17, 2000.

Williams, Stephanie. "Come Unglued." *Men's Health,* July 1, 1999.

Williams, Stephen. "Technophobia. Dear Victims of Electronic Progress: It's Time to Tame the Alien." *Newsday,* May 21, 1994.

Winans, Vanessa. "Can't Get it Out of My Head." *Toldeo Blade,* July 2, 2000.

Wineke, William. "He Put Your Nose Into His Business." *Wisconsin State Journal,* March 27, 1995.

Wollard, Kathy. *How Come?* New York: Workman Publishing, 1993.

————. "Itching To Know Why We Scratch." *Newsday,* July 30, 1996.

————. "Xmas isn't a Plot to take Christ out of Christmas." *Minneapolis Star Tribune,* December 21, 1997.

————. "You Can't Drive Without It. (Windshield Wiper)" *Weatherwise,* October 20, 1996.

Zelouf, David S. and Martin A. Posner. "Hand and wrist disorders: How to Manage Pain and Improve Function." *Geriatrics,* March 1, 1995.

Zoglin, Richard. "Video: Can Anybody Work This Thing?" *Time,* November 23, 1992.

————. "The Century Ahead: Beyond Your Wildest Dreams. TV Will Dazzle Us With Choices, But Will We Be Happy in Our Caccoons?", *Time,* October 15, 1992.

Zoroya, Gregg. "Passengers Behaving Badly." *USA Today,* November 19, 1999.